Simple Meanings of Legal Terms

Common Legal Terms for All

Kehinde Adegbite Esq.
LL.B., LL.M., BL.

(c) Kehinde Adegbite 2016

All rights reserved. No part of this book may be reproduced, stored or transmitted in any form or by any means, without prior permission of the copyright owner.

ISBN: 9798332633430

Dedication

This book is dedicated to God and Humanity.

Preface

The motivation to write this book came from those non-lawyers who, in spite of their loyalty and commitment to their own fields of discipline or areas of specialisation, continually make efforts to read legal texts either through the Internet or offline and in the course of time have acquired a good measure of legal terms. However, once in a while, they do use these terms wrongly. I wrote this book, therefore, to ease their efforts and to further expand their arsenal of legal words.

The language used in the book is simple and it is designed primarily for non-lawyers. Any averagely educated person can read and understand the book. While I cannot claim to have compiled an exhaustive list of legal terms that non-lawyers should learn and know, I have no doubt that an average reader will find the list here quite helpful and useful.

In case of any default, the responsibility is entirely mine.

Kehinde Adegbite Esq.
barrykehinde@yahoo.co.uk
www.kehindeadegbite.com.ng

Contents

Dedication
....
....

Preface
....
....

A – Z of Legal Terms
....

Simple Meanings of Legal Terms

A

AB INITIO – It simply means "from the beginning". It may be used to describe something that is faulty from its foundation. Usage – *"This case is bound to fail because it is defective ab initio."*

ABUSE OF COURT PROCESS – This encompasses a court action initiated against another person out of malice or for no just cause. Abuse of court process is also said to occur where a party duplicates court actions in order to harass an opponent. Such actions will be struck out as they amount to forum shopping.

ACCELERATED HEARING- This is an order given by a court in respect of a case which is meant to speed up the process of determining it. The order is usually made when a case has been in court for a long time or it is considered to deserve urgent determination and a case affected by this kind of order may be coming up in court on a daily basis or very frequently until it is finally decided. Courts usually give criminal cases accelerated hearing so as to decongest prisons, among others.

ACCEPTANCE – It means an unconditional agreement to the terms of a proposal (i.e. an offer made by one person to another). Once an offer is accepted, a contract comes into existence. The person accepting an offer is known as "offeree" while the person making it is called the "offeror". *Acceptance* is an important element in a contract.

ACCESSORY – This is a person who, though not present where a crime is committed, assists the offender in committing an offence. The assistance may come either before e.g. by giving an offender a piece of information which helps him to commit the offence or after the commission of the offence which may come by helping the offender to escape from being caught. So a person may be an *accessory* before the fact or *accessory* after the fact ("fact" is used here to mean an offence). An *accessory* is not a conspirator because he does not take part in the planning of the crime.

ACCOMPLICE[1] - This simply refers to a partner in crime. An *accomplice* is however not usually charged with the other suspect and is often used as a prosecution witness. (Compare: **ACCESSORY**)

ACCORD AND SATISFACTION – It is a kind of agreement which usually arises in relation to a contractual transaction where a party accepts what is less than what is due to him. For example, a creditor may decide to collect a lesser amount from a debtor who is unable to pay the full amount owed and therefore, release him from further obligation, having taken the lesser amount as the full and final settlement of his debt.

ACCUSATORIAL SYSTEM – It is a system of criminal trial where a judge is an umpire who must not take sides with either the prosecution or the defence. The judge allows the two sides to present their case as they want. This system does not allow a single person or body to be the judge and the prosecutor at the same time. This is the system in Nigeria.

ACCUSED PERSON – This is a person who has been charged to court to face trial for the offence he allegedly commits. He can only be called a criminal or convict after he has been tried and found guilty. He may also be referred to as a principal offender where there are other offenders.

---

[1]. Justice Belgore (J.S.C., rtd.) defined an accomplice in Okosi v. The State (1989) 1 CLRN 38 thus, "An accomplice is certainly a person that participates in a crime for which the accused now in court are being tried and if tried with them on the same evidence would equally be guilty with the accused being tried. In essence, an accomplice is not tried but if brought to trial along with other participes crimines, would become a co-accused person."

ACQUITTAL – This means a verdict of vindication entered in favour of a person who has been tried for a criminal act and found not guilty. (Compare: **DISCHARGED & ACQUITTED**)

ACT – This is a law made by the National Assembly as opposed to the one made by a State House of Assembly. An example is the Economic and Financial Crimes Commission Act, 2004. In fact, any law that ends with *"Act"* is deemed to have been made by the National Assembly.

ACTIO PERSONALIS MORITUR CUM PERSONA- This is a personal action which cannot survive a party to a law suit. In a law suit, an action is said to die and terminate with a party who dies while his case is yet to be finally decided. Instances are actions that border on defamation or negligence which are committed against a particular person. This principle does not, however, apply to a court action which borders on a party's property because such an action survives the party. If the party dies while the action is still on-going, his heirs may step into his shoes and continue with the case.

ACT OF GOD – It is an event which occurs exclusively due to natural causes without any form of human influence e.g. earthquake, tornado and so on. *Act of God* is capable of rendering a contract impossible to perform and therefore, no party will be held liable.

ACTUS REUS – This refers to a guilty act which one has performed. It is simply a criminal act i.e. the physical act of crime itself which may be stealing, rape, murder and so on. Where there is no *actus reus*, there is no crime committed.

ADEMPTION – This refers to a situation where a gift in a will is no longer in existence at the time of death of a testator and a beneficiary of such gift will not be able to take the benefit of it because it has *adeemed* (i.e. failed).

AD HOMINEM- It is a Latin word which has its origin in philosophy but that has found its way into legal dictionary. It means an argument which tends to attack the personality of an opponent instead of addressing the merits of the opponent's views.

AD INFINITUM – It means something going on without end. Usage – *"The community's suit against the company has been adjourned ad infinitum."*

ADJOURNMENT - It is a temporary postponement of a case to another date.

ADMISSIBLE EVIDENCE – This refers to a piece of evidence which the law allows a court to receive or take into consideration in its decision. Courts do not just admit evidence given before them but only pieces of evidence which comply with the laid-down rules. Evidence of a person who himself witnessed a case before a court is deemed an *admissible evidence* but hearsay evidence is inadmissible. (See, **HEARSAY EVIDENCE** below).

ADR – This simply stands for "alternative dispute resolution." It encompasses other means of settling disputes, other than litigation, such as negotiation, mediation, conciliation and arbitration. *ADR* is considered to be faster, less confrontational and cheaper, at least in the long run. This method of settling disputes only applies to civil conflicts or cases and not criminal matters.

ADVERSARIAL SYSTEM – This system applies to civil trials where parties to a case call and question witnesses while a judge takes the position of an unbiased arbiter.

AFFIDAVIT – It is a statement or declaration made under oath by a person called deponent or declarant. Everything written in an affidavit must be true and if it is not, it constitutes an offence known as perjury. Affidavit can be made for different purposes such as one made to correct the spelling of one's name or to declare one's age.

AFFIDAVIT OF SERVICE – It is a statement made under oath to show that a particular process of court has been served on the other party. This is usually prepared by a court bailiff.

AFFIRMATION – It is a declaration made by a witness in court pledging his readiness to speak the truth. Affirmation does not involve the taking of an oath but the witness is nevertheless bound to speak the truth. In practice, this only requires the witness to raise his hand without using any religious book to swear. This is usually allowed if a witness's religious belief prohibits the taking of an oath.

A FORTIORI- This is a process of reasoning in an argument which moves from a strong point to reach a conclusion.

AGENT – This is a person appointed by another person (better referred to as principal) to act on his behalf. The principal is responsible for all acts done by the *agent* within the scope of his instructions. If an *agent* acts outside his principal's instructions, he will be personally liable.

AGENT PROVOCATEUR – This is a person who wears a disguise to be part of a group of suspected people who are being secretly investigated or one who disguises to be a partner in crime with another person in order to gather evidence against that other person or persons being trailed for the purpose of criminal prosecution. An *agent provocateur* is usually a security agent who later gives evidence in court against the suspects that he has trailed.

AGE OF CONSENT – It is the age at which a girl can give consent to sexual intercourse. In Nigeria, this age is not clear in view of the controversial section 29 (4) (b) of the 1999 Constitution[2]. In the UK, the *age of consent* is 16.

AGE OF MAJORITY (also known as **FULL AGE**) - This is the legal age of adulthood by which a person can do a lot of things

---

[2]. Reading from section 29 (1) of the 1999 Constitution of Nigeria, it provides as follows: "Any citizen of Nigeria of full age who wishes to renounce his Nigerian citizenship shall make a declaration in the prescribed manner for the renunciation. (4) For the purposes of subsection (1) of this section- (a) 'full age' means the age of eighteen years and above; (b) any woman who is married shall be deemed to be of full age." (underline is mine).

legally. In Nigeria, this age ranges between 18 and 21. An eighteen year old person can vote but may not be eligible to vie for any political offices. A person of 18 years can also join in forming a company but cannot enter into a lot of other contracts. A person of 21 years, on the other hand, can get married even without parental consent, while any person below 21 must obtain parental consent in writing before he or she can enter into a marriage.

AIDING AND ABETTING – It is an act of assisting another person to commit a crime or to escape from being caught after the person has committed a crime. (Compare: **ACCESSORY**).

ALIMONY – This is an amount of money paid by a spouse (usually husband) to support the other spouse as ordered by a court of law on divorce. It may be a lump sum of money paid at once or on a continuing basis which may be monthly or any other interval as agreed between the parties or ordered by the court.

ALTER EGO – This simply means a person considered to be very close to another person or to an organisation. The term is normally used in a situation where there is need for court to call persons behind a corporate entity like a company to answer for their deeds. In other words, a company's *alter egos* are directors, stockholders and other officers.

ALLOCUTUS – It is a plea of leniency made by a person convicted of a crime in mitigation of punishment a court may impose on him[3].

AMENDMENT – It is a procedure by which papers already filed in court are modified, added to or subtracted from as the case may be. For example, a plaintiff who initially sues a defendant may later see reason to add some other persons as defendants in which case, an *amendment* becomes necessary.

---

[3]. The allocutus made by the late Chief Obafemi Awolowo during his trial for treasonable felony in 1962 remains a reference point to date. See, Awolowo O., MY MARCH THROUGH PRISON. 1985. Ibadan: Macmillan Nigeria Publishers Ltd. PP. 199-202.

AMICUS CURAE[4] – It means a friend of the court. This plays out when a lawyer or lawyers known to be very versatile are invited by a court to assist it by rendering their legal opinions on a matter in which they are not appearing for any of the parties.

AMNESTY- It is a form of pardon granted to a person who is undergoing a criminal trial. The pardon puts an end to his trial and sets him free. This power is usually exercised by states' Chief Judges and it only applies to persons alleged to have committed non-capital offences. (Compare: **PREROGATIVE OF MERCY**).

ANIMUS POSSIDENDI – It means a person's intention to possess something.

ANIMUS REVOCANDI – It means a person's intention to revoke, for instance, a will.

ANNULMENT- It is a legal process of cancelling or abrogating something that is considered to be invalid in the first place e.g. to annul an election that is alleged to be massively rigged or a marriage that is invalid from the onset. In the case of marriage, unlike divorce, annulling a marriage implies that the two parties involved in the marriage ought not to have married each other at all. This may happen where a person who is already married enters into a marriage under the Act with another person. Annulment is used where a marriage is a nullity, while divorce is the case where a valid marriage is terminated as a result of some problems which the two parties to the marriage consider unmanageable e.g. where one spouse deserts the other. However, childlessness is never a ground to dissolve a marriage.

APPEAL - It is a request made by a party to a higher court asking for the reversal of the judgment of a lower court. The right of a party to *appeal* against any decision that he is not pleased with is a constitutional right which means that nothing can take it away except

---

[4]. For a greater elaboration on its meaning, see, **Atake v. Afejuku (1994) 9 N.W.L.R. Pt. 368, 379**.

he decides not to exercise it. Decisions of every court are subject to *appeal* except those of the Supreme Court because by law whatever decision given by the Supreme Court is final.

APPEARANCE – It is the stage at which a lawyer announces to a court which of the parties he is representing, whether the plaintiff or the defendant. The lawyer will also introduce himself by mentioning his name. After a case is called and the parties who are in court have signified their presence, the next thing is for the lawyer to appear for his clients and where a litigant is unrepresented by a lawyer, he may also announce his *appearance*.

APPELLANT – This is a party who has filed an appeal against a judgement of a lower court before a higher court e.g. from the Court of Appeal to the Supreme Court.

APPELLATE COURT- This refers to any court which has power to handle an appeal from a lower court. Examples of *appellate courts* include the Supreme Court, Court of Appeal, State High Court and other superior Courts except the Federal High court that does not have powers to deal with appeals.

APPLICATION – Parties or their lawyers may have to make requests to a court at any stage of their case. These requests are technically called *applications*. *Application* may be oral or written. Most *applications* of serious implication are to be made in writing e.g. *application* to amend a court process.

APPLICANT- Any person making an application in a case is called an *applicant* whether the plaintiff (claimant) or the defendant. This is irrespective of whether the application is made orally or in writing.

A POSTERIORI (also known as **A PRIORI**) - This is a process of arguing from the cause to the effect.

ARBITRATION – It is a means by which a dispute is taken before an arbitrator (or arbitrators) instead of a court. This is done in order to save time and maintain a friendly business relationship.

ARBITRATOR – This is a person trained to settle disputes in a manner that is less formal in its procedure than the practice in regular courts. An *arbitrator* may be and may not be a lawyer but he is usually a person who is experienced in the subject-matter under consideration. He is expected to be neutral and impartial in his decision. There are usually two or three *arbitrators* presiding over a matter for arbitration.

ARBITRAL AWARD – Like a judgement given in a court matter, this is a decision made by an arbitrator in respect of a matter which has been submitted for arbitration. An *arbitral award* that is properly made is binding on the parties affected by it.

ARTIFICIAL PERSON – Companies are generally classified as *artificial persons* because they have almost every legal right that human beings have.

ARRAIGNMENT – This is the stage at which a suspect is taken before a court so as to read out an allegation to him and to give him opportunity to respond by saying whether he is guilty or not guilty. It must first take place in a criminal trial before witnesses can give their evidence.

ARTICLES OF ASSOCIATION- It is the document that sets out the rules regulating the internal workings of a company. Every company, whether public or private, must have *articles of association*.

ARTICLES OF PARTNERSHIP – It is a document that contains terms of agreement in a partnership business among partners. It may also be called DEED OF PARTNERSHIP. It is advisable that every partnership has its *articles of partnership*. Some of the basic contents of an article include the names of partners, the partners' addresses, mode of sharing profits, capital contribution, duration of the business, dissolution of the business and so on.

ASKING PRICE – It is a price at which a seller offers an article for sale which is usually subject to bargaining. The term is commonly used in connection with sales of landed property.

ASSAULT AND BATTERY – It is a kind of civil wrong (it could also be a crime[5]) which is committed when a person subjects another person to fear of being attacked (this is *assault*) and where the attack actually takes place, *battery* is said to be committed.

ASSENT – It refers to the signature of the President, Governors, or local government Chairmen to bring any law into force after law-makers at each level of government have passed such law.

ASSIGNMENT -It is the transfer of a person's ownership rights over some property, especially land, to another. It must be done by deed; hence, it is called DEED OF ASSIGNMENT.

AT LAW- It simply means according to law. It may also mean according to the Common Law as opposed to Equity.

ATTORNEY- This word may connote two things. It may mean an authorized agent appointed to act for another or a professional lawyer.

ATTORNEY-GENERAL – This is a lawyer appointed by either a state or the federal government as its chief law officer. For a person to be appointed as an *Attorney-General*, he must have been qualified as a lawyer for a period of not less than 10 years. He is the political head of the Ministry of Justice and offers advice to the government on legal matters. He is usually joined as a party in any suit where the government is being sued. In Nigeria, Attorney-General is also the Commissioner or Minister for Justice. It has been suggested in some quarters that the office of Attorney-General, whether at state or federal level, should not be joined with that of the Commissioner or Minister for Justice so as to ensure that an Attorney-General is a professional lawyer protecting the public interest while a

---

[5]. See, section 252 of the Criminal Code (supra).

Commissioner or Minister for Justice is a political appointee serving the interest of his appointor.

AUDI ALTERAM PARTEM – This simply means that all sides to a dispute must be heard or be given opportunity to be heard before a decision is taken affecting them one way or the other. In other words, it means to hear the other side. It is a mandatory constitutional requirement in any adjudicatory process and any failure to observe it renders such process null and void.

AUTREFOIS ACQUIT – This is a constitutional rule which states that a person who has been tried and found unblemished in respect of a crime must not be tried for the same offence again. For example, where it is alleged that **A** kills **B** and **A** is tried and found not guilty, then **A** cannot be tried for the murder of **B** again, except for the murder of **C** if that happens.

AUTREFOIS CONVICT – It is a counterpart of "autrefois acquit". This states that once a person is convicted of a particular crime, the same person cannot be convicted for the same offence again.

AVERMENTS (also known as **DEPOSITIONS**) - It means assertions, claims or statements made by a person in a legal document especially court papers e.g. affidavits and statement of claims. These assertions are usually made in paragraphs e.g. *"That I know as a fact that Mr Pik has been in detention since 10th Feb., 2013."*

B

BAIL – This is the act of releasing a person alleged to have committed a crime temporarily. A person may be released while investigation, trial or appeal is on-going.

BAIL BOND – This represents a monetary pledge which a surety makes in court in order to secure the bail of a suspect. Where the suspect is released on bail and he fails to attend court subsequently, the surety will have to pay the physical cash of the money pledged to the court and may also be detained until the suspect is found. If the suspect is later found, the surety will be released, while the suspect's bail would be cancelled.

BAILEE – This is a person who is given custody of some goods by another person known as bailor. The *bailee* does not have the ownership of the goods but mere custody of such goods until the bailor calls for their return.

BAILIFF - This is a court official whose main job is to serve papers issued by a court on whoever that needs to be served with such documents. He may also work with a Sheriff in order to enforce court orders.

BAILOR – This is a person who gives some goods to another person for safe-keeping or use. The *bailor* is the owner of the goods.

BANKRUPTCY – It is a process where a person may be declared bankrupt which connotes inability to pay debts. A bankrupt is a person who has been declared by a court as being unable to pay his debts. A company cannot be declared bankrupt. It is a real burden to be declared bankrupt because a bankrupt would be disqualified from holding certain political positions and he may remain so for 5 years unless he is able to off-set his debts before the expiration of the stated period.

BAR – It means a body of lawyers. It is used to represent lawyers as an association. It may also be used in relation to a ceremony where newly qualified lawyers are formally admitted into the league of their professional colleagues. Usage – *"Newly-qualified lawyers are being called to the **Bar** today."* Furthermore, the word *"bar"* may equally be used to describe where lawyers sit and stand to address a judge or magistrate in a court-room.

BARRISTER – He is a lawyer who, having passed the required professional examinations, is authorized to represent other people in a law court as their advocate. In the Nigerian context, the following words – lawyer, legal practitioner, advocate, attorney, counsel and solicitor - are used interchangeably.

BENCH – It is used to refer to a body of judges. Once a lawyer is appointed to the *Bench*, he can no longer practise in terms of appearing in court for clients especially a high court judge. A body of magistrates is referred to as the lower *Bench*, while a body of judges is called the higher *Bench*.

BENCH RULING - This is a decision which a judge or magistrate gives in respect of a case without retiring to his chambers (office) before doing so. He writes and delivers it in the open court.

BENCH WARRANT – It is an order of court issued for the purpose of bringing before a court a person who has failed to attend court after he has been granted bail or an order for the arrest of a fleeing suspect. (See, **JUMP BAIL**).

BENEFICIAL OWNER – This is a person who enjoys the benefits of ownership in a particular property, even though the legal title of the property resides with another person. An example is the relationship between a beneficiary in a will/trust and a trustee. While the beneficiary is the equitable owner, the trustee is regarded as the legal owner. (See, my book: HOW TO WRITE YOUR WILL WITH EASE for details).

BEQUEST – It refers to a gift of a personal (movable) item in a will other than immovable gift such as land or house.

BIGAMY – It is an offence which is committed when a person who has married in accordance with the English law enters into another marriage under the Act while the first marriage remains undissolved. This offence attracts 7 years' imprisonment. It should be stressed that the offence may be committed by both sexes.

BILATERAL CONTRACT - This is a contract that involves two parties.

BILL OF EXCHANGE – It is a commercial paper which constitutes an order to whom it is addressed to pay money to a named person.

BILL OF LADING - It is a document issued to a transporter of goods which validates his rights to hold those goods for the time being and which also indicates the person (s) to whom the goods are to be delivered. This document usually accompanies goods in transit whether by road or by sea.

BINDING AUTHORITY – A judgement of a higher court is said to have binding effect on a lower court if the facts of a case being handled by the lower court are similar to the facts of the case already decided by the higher court. In other words, a *binding authority* is a case that must be followed by a lower court in deciding a present case before it.

BINDING OVER - It is an order of a magistrate court asking a suspect to keep peace and behave orderly. This kind of order is usually issued in a case of breach of peace or violence by demanding an accused person to stop the act of violence instead of committing him to prison.

BODY OF BENCHERS - This is the highest regulatory body for the practice of legal profession in Nigeria and it also certifies persons who are to be admitted as legal practitioners into the Nigerian Bar. The body is constituted by eminent lawyers and has the Chief Justice of Nigeria as its current chairman.

BONA FIDE – It simply means good faith. The term is normally used in relation to certain transactions or relationships that require highest level of honesty among the parties involved such as principal/agent and the insurer/the insured.

BONA VACANTIA – It encapsulates abandoned individual property which government takes over as no owner or relations of such owner is laying claim to it.

BORSTAL INSTITUTION - It is a place set up by the government to detain underage children (below 18 years old) who have committed a crime, for some length of time which may not be more than 3 years. During this period, they are made to learn some vocations or undergo educational training. There are three borstal institutions in Nigeria and they are in Kaduna, Abeokuta and Ilorin. (Compare: **REMAND HOME**).

BREVI MANU - It means "summarily".

BRIDE PRICE - It is the money, goods or property given by a bridegroom or his family to the family of a bride which usually forms part of the requirements for marriage. (Contrast: **DOWRY**). The payment of bride price is compulsory under Customary law but it is not so under the Marriage Act (also known as English law).

BRIEF – This may be used to qualify the instructions given to a lawyer by a client. On the other hand, it may mean a body of argument which is prepared in respect of an appeal. It is usually called Brief of Argument.

BROKEN-DOWN IRRETRIEVABLY – The phrase is normally used to describe a marriage which has deteriorated beyond remedy. Once a party suing for divorce is able to satisfy a court that his matrimony with the other party has so degenerated that the only option is for the marriage to be dissolved, the court is more likely to dissolve such marriage.

BURDEN OF PROOF (also known as **ONUS OF PROOF**) - It refers to the task that a party bears in a case to prove certain facts. This simply illustrates a common saying that *"he who asserts must prove"*.

BYE-LAW – This is a law or regulation made by a local government council, judicial or executive branch of government such as commissioner, minister or agency. *Bye-laws* may also be called subsidiary regulation, delegated or secondary legislation.

C

CALL OUT OF TURN – This is a practice where cases are mentioned in court by lawyers, usually in the order of their seniority, without following how cases appear on the cause list.

CALL-OVER DATE – This is used to describe cases that fall on public holidays as a result of which they do not come up as courts would not sit. Such cases would first be attended to when next courts sit before cases of that particular day are called.

CAPITAL OFFENCE – It is an offence which attracts death as its punishment. Examples of *capital offences* are murder, armed robbery and treason.

CASE LAW – It is a body of judgments delivered by courts. It is also known as Common Law or Judicial Authority. It is simply a statement or principle of law that is established through a decided case. For instance, **Salomon vs. Salomon & Co. Ltd (1897)** is the *case law* for the principle of corporate personality of a company.

CASE TO ANSWER - It is a ruling of court which confirms that the prosecution's case against an accused person is not baseless, though this is not a ruling finding the accused person guilty yet. It simply requires the accused person to enter his defence in response to the prosecution's case against him.

CAUSE OF ACTION – It captures the totality of events which entitles one person to sue another in a court of law. In order to bring any action to court, it must be clear that certain events have taken place which call for court intervention. If it does not, such a case will be rejected (struck out) by court. Let us assume that an employee is, by letter of employment, entitled to a month's notice before his employer may terminate his employment. Recently, he is told by fellow employees that their employer is planning to terminate his employment without notice. If he files an action, only because of what he has heard from other workers, to stop his employer from dismissing him without the required notice, the action is bound to be struck out for lack of a *cause of action*.

CAUSE LIST (BAR LIST) - It is a list containing all the cases before a court whether for a week or in a day. It helps lawyers and litigants to know in advance before the court sits whether or not their matters are coming up that day or week as the case may be and if they are coming up, to know what they are coming up for, whether for hearing or mention.

CAVEAT – It simply means a formal warning. This formal warning may be entered in a newspaper in order to stop an imminent sale of a particular property in which the person entering the *caveat* has interest. It may be also used to stop the issuance of letters of administration.

CAVEAT EMPTOR – It means "let the buyer beware." This rule requires a buyer to be watchful and careful in his transactions in order to ensure that what he buys conforms to his specification.

CAVEAT VENDITOR - It means "let the seller beware." It is a rule which demands of sellers to sell goods of required standards to buyers. Unless there is a disclaimer to the knowledge of a buyer, a seller is liable for selling goods of low quality.

CERTIFIED TRUE COPY – It represents official mark on a document which authenticates the document as a true copy of its original. Documents may be certified in courts or by a notary public.

CERTIORARI – This is a kind of form issued by a higher court to a lower court requiring the latter to bring its proceedings before it for the purpose of determining whether the lower court has exceeded its powers in relation to a matter or not. If it is found that the lower court has exceeded its power, the higher court may set aside such proceedings. This may happen between a magistrate court and high court.

CETERIS PARIBUS – It means "all other factors or things remaining the same." Usage- "Mr. Joe may soon be appointed a Senior Advocate of Nigeria, ceteris paribus."

CHARGE AND BAIL – This phrase is commonly used derogatively to describe lawyers whose main pre-occupation is to loiter around courts' premises so as to enjoy the patronage of suspects who do not have their own lawyers. Whenever these suspects are brought to court by the police, these lawyers solicit to appear for them so as to apply for their bail at some ridiculous amount. This practice of law is unethical and it does not paint the profession in a good light. A practice akin to this in the U.S is called "Ambulance Chasing[6]" and lawyers who do it are referred to as "Ambulance Chasers".

CHARGE SHEET – This is the document, mostly prepared by the Police at the magistrate courts, which contains information as to which offence an accused person is charged with, the time and place the crime is committed. It also contains the name of the victim. It basically gives suspect information about the case against him.

---

[6]. For details, see, "Ambulance Chancer", available online at http://www.duhaime.org/LegalDictionary/A/AmbulanceChaser.aspx (accessed on 30th June, 2014).

CIVIL LAW – This may connote two things. One, it means a legal system which is different from the Common Law System. An example of a country with the *Civil Law* System is France. The second meaning is to see *civil law* as a body of rules which regulates such subject-matters as contract, employment, company matters, torts and so on. In this sense, *civil law* may be contrasted with criminal law which imposes punishments on offenders. *Civil law* does not aim to punish wrong-doers in terms of a party who breaches his responsibilities in relation to a contract. However, it may impose non-punitive reliefs such as damages, injunction, e.t.c. Again, a civil matter usually has a lifespan. For instance, if two people have a contractual dealing and there is need for either of them to take a legal action, unless the action is taken within six months or a year, the right to take such action may become expired. (See, **STATUTE-BARRED ACTION** or **STATUTE OF LIMITATION**).

CIRCUMSTANTIAL EVIDENCE – It is a piece of evidence which is based on inference rather than personal knowledge or experience. For example, **A** is stabbed to death in his own apartment while **B** is seen by some people some minutes after the stabbing rushing out of **A's** apartment with blood stains all over him. If the evidence of the people that saw **B** rushing out of **A's** apartment is all that is before the court, it will be difficult for **B** to come out from the kind of incriminating inference which the trial court may draw from this *circumstantial evidence*. Even though courts rarely depend on circumstantial evidence to convict an accused person, a court may rely on it if it is strong and points to an irresistible conclusion that the accused person commits the crime.

CITATION - It is the method by which lawyers provide to the court a reference of cases which they are relying on in respect of cases they handle before that court. For example, a reference to a case as *"Onuoha v. State"* is incomplete unless the following additional information *"(1998) 13 NWLR Pt. 583, 531"* is provided which is actually the *citation* of the referred case.

CLAIMANT – It is a party who commences a law suit against another in a civil claim. *Claimant* may also be referred to as plaintiff.

CLASS ACTION - It is a case filed by a group of people who have a common cause. For example, a case filed by all subscribers of a telecommunication company having complaints about poor service and arbitrary tariffs on calls they made is a good specimen of a *class action*. In a class action, unlike representative action, parties suing as plaintiffs may not be ascertainable. They may simply be described by their common cause and their individual names may not appear on court papers. In fact, the plaintiffs may not know themselves. (Compare: **REPRESENTATIVE ACTION**).

CLIENT – This is a person who engages a lawyer to perform certain tasks for him whether it involves appearing in court for him or not.

CODICIL – It simply means a supplement to a will. It may also be used to correct a will in any **manner.**

COLLECTIVE AGREEMENT (also known as **COLLECTIVE BARGAINING AGREEMENT**) – It is an agreement entered into by employers and employees or their union in relation to the conditions of service of employees. It spells out the duties and rights of each side of the bargain. It is usually in writing and signed by the parties to it.

COMMISSIONER FOR OATHS - This is an official of court whose task is to administer oath and sign documents made under oath.

COMMON LAW - This system of law originated from Britain and it is also found commonly with countries that were formerly under the British colonial administration. This system is based essentially on the principle of judicial precedent.

COMMON SEAL (also known as **COMPANY SEAL**) - It is a stamp used by companies in order to signify their signature on documents. Whenever a company is a party to a transaction which is contained in a document, especially formal contracts, the company must sign by stamping it with its *common seal*.

COMMUNITY SERVICE- It is a form of punishment imposed on a person who has been tried by a court of law and found guilty of a crime(s). The punishment is non-custodial in which case the offender is not confined to a prison. He stays in his community and is placed under the supervision of a Community Service Officer who has a duty to ensure that the offender performs such services as environmental sanitation, attending to the needs and care of children and the elderly in government-approved homes and so on. In Nigeria, Lagos State[7] is the only state that provides for this kind of punishment.

COMPANY – This is a business organization which has been duly registered in line with the provisions of law. In Nigeria, the law regulating the registration of companies is the Companies and Allied Matters Act, 2004 (shortened as CAMA). A *company* is an artificial person.

COMPOS MENTIS - It refers to a state of sound mental condition. (Contrast: **NON COMPOS MENTIS** below).

COMPLAINANT – This may be used to refer to a person who lodges a criminal complaint against another at a police station or to refer to a victim of a criminal act. It may also be used to refer to the government where the latter has commenced a criminal trial against a suspect.

COMPLAINT - It may be used to qualify a court paper which is filed in commencing a criminal case in the high court or a paper used to initiate a civil action in magistrate courts.

---

[7]. See, section 347 of the Administration of Criminal Justice Law of Lagos State, 2011. See also, Bob Osamor, CRIMINAL PROCEDURE LAWS AND LITIGATION PRACTICES. 2012. (Second Edition) Manchester: Dee-Sage (Books+ Prints) P.498.

COMPOUNDING A FELONY – This is a crime which may be committed by a victim of another crime. Assume **A** is raped by **B**. **B** has been charged with the offence of rape but **A** is being pressurized to drop the complaint against **B**. If **A** agrees and tries to withdraw the complaint, then **A** may also be charged with the offence of *compounding a felony* because it is an offence to withdraw serious crimes of which rape is one.

CONCURRENT SENTENCE – It is a method of punishment employed where a person is found guilty of multiple crimes with varying degrees of punishments and the terms of imprisonment are to run simultaneously (i.e. together or at the same). For example, **A** is standing trial for 3 different crimes with each carrying the following jail terms: 4, 7 and 2 years' imprisonment respectively. Where **A** is found guilty of all the three counts and the trial judge allows the terms to run together (i.e. concurrently), then it means **A** will only spend 7 years in prison because that is the highest jail term and not 13 years. Similarly, assuming each of the 3 offences carries the same jail term, say 5 years. In that case, **A** will only serve 5 years in prison and not 15 years. (Contrast: **CONSECUTIVE SENTENCE**).

CONCURRING JUDGEMENT – This is a judgment which agrees with another judgment (i.e. the supposed majority/lead judgment of a particular court). This happens mainly in the Supreme Court, Court of Appeal and Election Petition Tribunals. This is because all these courts have more than a judge presiding over them while a judgment supported by a larger number of judges in any of these courts is regarded as the majority or lead judgment, other judges too have to write their individual judgments (otherwise known as *concurring judgment*) where they will clearly state their agreement with the majority judgment. (Contrast: **DISSENTING JUDGMENT** below).

CONDITION PRECEDENT - It is a step that has to be taken before the doing of a particular thing e.g. before filing a law suit. For example, serving a quit notice on a tenant is a condition precedent to the ejection of the tenant or filing an action in court for the purpose of ejecting him.

CONDONATION - It means forgiveness. In matrimonial matters, it means a situation where a spouse forgives the other spouse of a misconduct e.g. adultery which could have formed a basis for the innocent spouse to bring an action for the dissolution of their marriage. The forgiveness is made on the basis that the spouse who does wrong would not repeat the wrongful act in future. However, once a spouse condones the wrongful act of the other spouse, the innocent spouse cannot subsequently bring an action for divorce over the same wrong that has originally been condoned.

CONFESSIONAL STATEMENT – It is a statement made at the police station by a suspect in which he voluntarily confesses to the commission of the alleged crime. For a *confessional statement* to be useful for the purpose of prosecuting its maker it must have been made willingly and the confession must relate to the instant crime allegedly committed by the suspect not another crime which is different from the one before the court for which he is being charged.

CONSANGUINITY – It means blood relationship. Under the Marriage Act, there are people within certain degrees of blood relationship that are not permitted to be joined as husband and wife. However, this restraint may be by-passed if a marriage is celebrated under another law other than the English Law. For example, first cousins cannot be married under the English Law.

CONSECUTIVE SENTENCE – This is a sentencing which requires a person convicted of more than one crime to serve the punishment of each crime one after the other, unlike concurrent sentence.

CONSENSUS AD IDEM – This is normally used in a contract to connote that parties to a contract are in agreement as to terms of their relationship. Usage - *"It can be said that we are all at **consensus ad idem** in relation to how the road construction project is to be performed."*

CONSENT JUDGMENT – This is a judgment made by a court which is based on terms of settlement as drawn up by parties to an amicable settlement. Whenever *consent judgment* is made, it means parties who are already in court have been able to explore the option of settling their dispute among themselves and thereafter bring the outcome of their settlement for court approval.

CONSIDERATION – This is one of the elements of a valid contract which simply means what a party gives in return for what he gains in such a contract. For instance, **A** sells his wristwatch to **B** for N5, 000. In this instance, both **A** and **B** have given *consideration.* **A**'s *consideration* is the watch which he gives up while **B**'s *consideration* is the money which he pays. So *consideration* connotes gain and loss.

CONSPIRACY - It is an offence which is committed when two or more persons plan and carry out a criminal act. Here, parties agree to do an unlawful act or a lawful act by unlawful means.

CONSPIRATOR - This is a partner in crime who, along with some other offenders, plans the commission of a crime. He may and may not be physically present at the scene of crime. He bears the same degree of punishment as the principal offender.

CONSTITUTIONAL SUPREMACY – It is a principle which states that the provisions of the constitution are superior to any other law of the land. It states further that if any other law is inconsistent with the constitution, such contravening section or law will be null and void. This concept also means that every person, whether citizens or government officials, is bound by the provisions of the constitution.

CONSUMMATION – It is the act of completing a marriage with the first act of sexual intercourse after a wedding ceremony. Failure to have the first act of sexual intercourse after the wedding ceremony, especially if it does not take place, say a year after, is a ground to seek for dissolution of marriage. However, there may not be a basis for dissolution if the lack of *consummation* is as a result of the agreement of the couple. On the other hand, if a spouse is ready and willing for *consummation* and the other is refusing and it continues for some time, the party who is willing may file for dissolution of the marriage.

CONSUMER PROTECTION – This refers to the totality of efforts of the government in the forms of laws and agencies which are meant to ensure that consumers have value for whatever article they purchase. It was in the pursuit of protecting Nigerian Consumers that the government established Consumer Protection Council with the mandate of eradicating adulterated, fake, inferior and hazardous products from market places.

CONTEMPT OF COURT – This is an act of disrespect to the court which may be either in the face of the court or disrespect shown to an order of court. *Contempt of court* is a punishable act which terms of punishment depend on whether the contempt is criminal or civil. Civil contempt carries 6 months' imprisonment, while criminal contempt is 3 months.

CONTENTIOUS APPLICATION – An application made in court is said to be contentious when the other side is opposing it.

CONTRACT FOR SERVICE – This is a relationship between an employer (client) and an independent contractor. This kind of contract does not create an employer and an employee relationship because none of the two parties has control over the other. The relationship between a passenger and a cab-driver is an example of a *contract for service*.

CONTRACT OF SERVICE – This is a relationship between an employer and employee and in this kind of relationship, the employee is subject to the control of the employer. Examples of this relationship abound e.g. Oyo State Government and the state civil servants. The employer dictates how the work should be done, time to resume and to close and how much pay to receive, e.t.c.

CONTRA PROFERENTEM RULE – This is a principle under the law of contract which states that whenever a party to a contract inserts a clause into the contract and the meaning of the clause is unclear, the unclear clause would be interpreted against the interest of the party that inserts it. The purpose of this rule is to protect the interest of the other party against whom the clause is inserted in the first place.

CONTRIBUTORY NEGLIGENCE – This concept usually arises in a case of negligence where a person (defendant) sued for negligence is not denying liability but is saying that the claimant also contributes to the occurrence of the negligence.

CONVERSION – This is a civil wrong which is committed where a non-owner of goods is exercising some rights over the goods as if he is the owner. *Conversion* is not stealing because while stealing is a crime, the former is a civil wrong. (Compare: **DETINUE**)

CONVICT (CRIMINAL) - This refers to a suspect who has been found guilty of committing a crime.

CONVICTION – It is a finding of guilt made against an accused person before punishment is imposed. In determining the fate of an accused person, at the point of delivering a judgement, a court's judgement is usually in two parts. One aspect will pronounce the guilt of the accused person while the second part will pronounce the nature of punishment whether fine, imprisonment or death to be imposed. The first part is otherwise known as *conviction*. (Compare: **SENTENCING**).

COPYRIGHT- It means a person's exclusive enjoyment of what he has created which entitles him to prevent others from copying his original works. Works which deserve this kind of protection include books, music, films and other creations of art.

CORAM - It is normally used to indicate which judge is handling or handled a matter. For example, *"**Coram**: Adegbite J."* This indicates Justice Adegbite.

CORPUS DELICTI – This Latin expression word is normally used to denote a physical evidence of a crime e.g. a corpse in a murder case. The term is restrictively used in connection with the offence of murder.

CORPUS JURIS – It means "a body of law." Usage – *"The new book written by Justice Niki Tobi can simply be regarded as the Nigerian **corpus juris**."*

CORONER'S COURT - It is a special court established solely to conduct coroner inquests when necessary. It is usually a magistrate court.

CORONER - This is an officer of court usually a magistrate charged with the responsibility of conducting investigation (technically called *coroner* inquest) into the cause of death of a particular individual whose death must have occurred as a result of violence or through a mysterious circumstance or so sudden that it raises some suspicion.

CORONER'S INQUEST - It is an exercise by which a coroner conducts an investigation into the cause of death of any person. This is usually done where death occurs in a suspicious circumstance. It is a common practice to conduct *coroner's inquest* for persons who die in prisons.

CORROBORATING EVIDENCE – This is a piece of evidence coming from a witness which supports or confirms the evidence earlier given by another witness in a matter before a court of law. There are instances where it is compulsory or safe to have this corroborating evidence before a decision is made especially in criminal cases and some of such instances are in a case of rape or defilement where the victim is a minor or the only evidence before a court is that of an accomplice.

COST – It is a sum of money awarded in a civil case which is meant to take care of out of pocket expenses of either the lawyer or the client receiving it. (Contrast with **DAMAGES**, below).

COUNTER-AFFIDAVIT – It is an affidavit which contains facts disputing a set of facts in another affidavit. Once an affidavit has been made and there is need to contest the contents of such affidavit, it requires a *counter-affidavit* to do it.

COUNTER-CLAIM – It represents a paper filed in court by a defendant to make a claim (or claims) in a suit where he is being sued by a plaintiff. This means that the person filing a *counter-claim* is both a defendant and a plaintiff in the same case and may also be called a counter-claimant.

COUNTERMAND ORDER - It means a cancellation or revocation of a previous instruction. This is used to qualify a counter order given by a customer to his bank instructing it not to honour a cheque which he has previously issued to a particular person. For a *countermand order* to be effective, it has to be in writing and given by the same person who originally issues the cheque and not his agent. It has to be submitted before the initial order has been carried out.

COUNTER-OFFER – A *counter-offer* is said to occur where an offer, which should be accepted without any modification, is accepted by a person to whom an offer is made on terms other than the terms on which the offer is proposed. For example, **A** offers to sell his Blackberry phone to **B** for N25, 000 and **B** responds by expressing his willingness to pay N18, 000 for the phone. The N18, 000 offered by **B** here is regarded as a counter-offer and it becomes an offer in itself which may either be accepted or rejected by **A**.

COURT OF FIRST INSTANCE - This refers to any court that the law gives power (jurisdiction) to start a case from the beginning i.e. before which court a case should be commenced. It can also be said that it is a court that has original jurisdiction to try a matter. For instance, a case that has to do with wrongful dismissal of an employee must be commenced before the National Industrial Court because it is the court of first instance in respect of labour matters. Where a case is commenced before a court that does not have original jurisdiction, the case would be struck out for want of jurisdiction.

COURT OF SUMMARY JURISDICTION - It is a court empowered by law to try both civil and criminal cases in a speedier manner than it would have been if taken to a higher court. Magistrate courts are *courts of summary jurisdiction* because their procedures for trials are not as elaborate as States' High Courts. Federal High Court is also a court of summary jurisdiction in relation to criminal matters. Where, for instance, an accused person pleads (i.e. admits) guilty to a crime, a court of summary jurisdiction can immediately (summarily) convict him without further trial.

COURT PROCESS - This encompasses all court papers that may be filed in a case e.g. motions and affidavits. For a non-lawyer, *court process* may appear to have the same meaning as pleadings but one is wider in scope than the other. While *court process* includes all court papers in respect of any case, pleadings are limited to processes like statement of claim, statement of defence and few others. (Compare: **PLEADINGS**).

COURT PROCEEDINGS – It encompasses all the activities that take place in courts from the point at which a case is filed to the stage a judgement is delivered.

COVENANTS – This word is often used to qualify terms in a land sale agreement and other documents having to do with the transfer of interest over land or landed property. These terms capture what parties to such documents may do or may not do, for example, a term placing an obligation on a seller of property to indemnify a buyer where a third party is challenging the rights of the buyer over the property.

CRIMINAL LAW – It is a body of law which defines offences and also stipulates punishments for them. It may also be defined as a body of law which seeks to protect the collective interest of a community against certain behaviours or conducts that threaten their communal existence e.g. murder, rape, armed robbery and so on. Most criminal cases do not have limitation period or time limit. A crime committed many years ago may still be prosecuted, if there is still evidence to prove it.

CROSS-EXAMINATION – It is a process in which an opponent is putting questions to the other party or the other party's witness (es) in order to obtain responses which are favourable to his own side. The opponent may also want to put questions which would elicit answers that are contrary to whatever the other party has earlier said so as to portray the party being cross-examined as a liar who the court should not believe. *Cross-examination* is a weapon used by lawyers to achieve favourable result for their clients in a court case. Cross-examiners usually frame their questions in a manner that answers would come in either "yes" or "no" fashion. A wise witness, on the other hand, will find a way of supplying additional information even when he has answered in a "yes" or "no" manner.

CUSTODY MATTER - This is used to refer to criminal cases in which accused persons are not on bail and which courts usually give some priority over other cases so that the prisoners would know their fate on time.

D

DAMAGE – It means an injury or harm which a person has suffered for which there is a legal remedy. It is not every type of *damage* that can be remedied at law. For instance, a business person whose business folds up because of aggressive marketing strategies of his competitors cannot find any succour in court for any *damage* he may have suffered as a result.

DAMAGES – It is a monetary compensation awarded by a court of law in favour of a victorious party. *Damages* can only be awarded if a party asks for it, though the court may grant an amount lower than the one asked for but it cannot be higher.

DAMNUM SINE INJURIA - It means "damage without legal injury". This refers to an injury which a person has suffered but for which there is no remedy at law. For example, if a person is driven out of business as a result of stiff competition from his business opponents, though an injury has been suffered, the law does not provide any remedy for such unfortunate business person. It is an injury but not a legal injury.

DEBENTURE HOLDER – This is a person who has given some loan to a company and he is therefore a creditor to that company. He earns interests on the loan.

DEBENTURE – It is a document issued to its holder to show that a particular company is indebted to him. It is basically a document acknowledging a company's indebtedness to its holder.

DECREE – This may mean a law made by the highest law-making body in a military government e.g. Detention of Persons Decree No. 2 of 1984. The word *"decree"* may also be used to connote a court order.

DECREE ABSOLUTE – This is a final order usually in a divorce case. Once this order is made, the parties are free to re-marry. It is also applicable to garnishee proceedings.

DECREE NISI – This is an order of court usually in a divorce case which is made temporary in order to give the couple more opportunity to settle their differences amicably before a final order (otherwise known as **DECREE ABSOLUTE**) is made. *Decree nisi* is normally given a life span of 3 months before it becomes absolute.

DEED - This refers to a formal document of special nature. Certain agreements are required by law to be made by deed in order for them to be valid e.g. a document to prove ownership of land.

DEED OF ASSENT - Whenever a will (even including letters of administration) is made and some landed property is being given through such will, a legal document must subsequently be prepared by the executors of the will which would formally transfer the ownership of any landed property in that will to a beneficiary. Deed of Assent is the legal document through which this can be done.

DEED OF GIFT - It is a legal document usually prepared to transfer property, especially landed property e.g. land, to another person as a gift or whenever the receiver is not required to pay either in cash or in kind for what is being given to him. Any other property may be given to a person as a gift without the use of Deed of Gift but this is not so where land or other landed property is to be transferred. If a gift of landed property is intended to be legally valid, it must be done with a Deed of Gift. The document is better prepared by a lawyer.

DEED OF PARTITION - It is a legal document in which property, formerly owned jointly by some people usually a family, is shared, dividing it into portions and transferring each portion to individual owners. This is usually done in a situation where a family decides to share family land or house among their family members.

DE FACTO – It is normally used to depict a real situation of things which, though may not be legal and legitimate, has to be accepted for all practical purposes. Usage – *"Adly Mansour became the **de facto** president of Egypt as a result of unconstitutional change of government."*

DEFAULT JUDGEMENT – This is a judgment made as a result of non-appearance of a defendant in court. Where a defendant is aware of a suit against him and refuses to appear in court nor does he file any document, the court may enter a judgment in his absence.

DEFENCE COUNSEL - This is a lawyer defending a suspect in a criminal trial.

DEFENDANT – It is a person sued in a civil case. An accused person in a criminal case may also be referred to as *defendant*.

DE JURE – This is used to describe a position occupied as of right or in accordance with law. Usage – *"Having won in a free and fair election, he is the **de jure** Governor."*

DELEGATED LEGISLATION – It represents regulations which are made by other arms of government other than the legislature.

DELEGATUS NON POTEST DELEGARE – It simply means that a person who is exercising powers on behalf of another person cannot appoint another person to act for him. For instance, an agent is a delegate of a principal so he cannot appoint another agent to act for him without a clear authority of his principal permitting him to do so.

DEMAND LETTER - It is a letter written by a creditor to his debtor in order to request for the payment of money owed. Such letter usually gives a time-frame within which the debtor has to make payment so as to avoid a court action. In some cases, such letters must first be written before a creditor can sue even when there is need to do so.

DE MINIMIS - (in full it is written as **DE MINIMIS NON CURAT LEX**) It means "the law cares not for small things". It is a principle by which courts refuse to be drawn into frivolous issues. For example, a court, on the basis of this principle, may refuse to entertain a dispute which borders on hot exchanges between two people.

DEPONENT (also called **DECLARANT** or **AFFIANT**) - It is used to qualify any person who makes an affidavit and signs it as the person who makes the statement contained in the affidavit.

DESERTION - It is a situation where a spouse abandons the other spouse without the latter's consent and without known reason for a period of time. If the abandonment continues for a year, the other spouse may sue for divorce.

DETINUE - It is a civil wrong where a person detains another person's goods or personal property for no just cause, even when the owner has formally requested for it to be returned. This is also known as unlawful detention.

DIRECT EVIDENCE – This is, in other words, an eye-witness account of an event. A witness gives *direct evidence* by stating what he sees, hears, touches or perceives. It is a piece of evidence which emanates from what the witness personally experiences other than information obtained from another person.

DIRECTORS – These are persons appointed by a company to direct and manage the affairs of such company.

DIRECTOR OF PUBLIC PROSECUTIONS – This is a director in the Ministry of Justice either at the state or federal level who heads the department of public prosecutions. It is this department that co-ordinates all criminal cases especially serious ones which the police are usually, in practice, excluded from prosecuting. The *Director of Public Prosecution* (shortened as DPP) is the one that initiates criminal prosecutions at the State or Federal High Court as the case may be. The director is a career officer who is also a lawyer. He does not, however, engage in investigation of crimes which is squarely the duty of security agents to do especially the police.

DISCHARGE – This term is normally used in relation to a person who is standing for a criminal trial but has been set free, though not on account of being tried and found not guilty. An accused person may be *discharged* if there are no witnesses to give evidence in his case. A person discharged may still be re-arrested and tried if new facts emerge. The word *"discharge"* may also be used to mean the act of terminating a contract and one's employment.

DISCHARGED AND ACQUITTED - It is an order of court which totally frees a suspect who has been tried and found not guilty of the alleged crime. Once an accused person is discharged and acquitted, he cannot be re-arrested and re-tried for that same offence.

DISCLAIM/DISCLAIMER - It is a clause in a document which tries to exclude a party who inserts it from liability in case any arises in relation to the transaction that the document covers.

DISMISSAL – It is the act of sacking an employee from his job by his employer due to a breach of terms of his employment or a commission of an act which amounts to gross misconduct. A dismissed employee is not entitled to terminal benefits e.g. gratuity. (Compare: **TERMINATION**).

DISMISSING A CASE – A case is said to have been dismissed when witnesses have given evidence or lawyers have argued and a decision taken which states that the case does not have any merit. Once a case is dismissed, the decision is final and could only be appealed against. (See, **FINAL JUDGEMENT**).

DISSENTING JUDGEMENT – This is a minority judgment in which a different result is arrived at as opposed to the lead/majority judgment. However, a *dissenting judgment* is a mere opinion of the dissenting judge. It does not represent the judgment of the court. (Compare: **CONCURRING JUDGMENT**).

DISTINGUISH – This is a situation where a lower court avoids following a previous decision of a higher court due to the lower court's ability to show that the facts of the present case before it are different from the facts of the case previously decided by the higher court. What this means is that the principle of judicial precedent may not be observed where a lower court is able to differentiate the case before it from the one being referred to.

DOCK – It is a box, usually wooden, in which an accused person in a case stands in courts in order to follow the case against them. It may be located directly opposite a judge or magistrate or any other place in a court-room.

DOCTRINE OF NECESSITY - It is a principle which permits a government to act in a way, as a result of an emergency situation, that would not have been allowed in a normal circumstance. This played in 2010 when the National Assembly empowered Dr. Jonathan, then the Nigerian Vice President to become Acting President even though the Constitution did not expressly provide for that.

DONATIO MORTIS CAUSA – It is a gift of property made to a person while the owner is in a situation where death is expected or appears imminent.

DOWRY - This refers to property or gifts brought by a bride from her parents' house to her husband's house at marriage. (Contrast: **BRIDE PRICE**).

DRAWEE – This refers to a bank on which a customer has issued a cheque requesting the bank to pay a specified sum of money.

DRAWER – This is an account holder i.e. a bank customer who issues a cheque whether in his name or for another person requesting his bank to pay a specified sum of money to the person whose name is written on the cheque.

DUE DILIGENCE – It means a process of following laid-down rules and procedures in carrying out an act. It may relate to compliance with acceptable standards in awarding contracts or in executing government projects.

DUPLICATE CASE-FILE – This is a case file that contains all the details of police investigation in respect of a criminal incident which has been reported to the police. In this file, all the statements made by the complainant and witnesses to the crime, if any, statements of the suspects, items recovered from the suspects if any and so on would be compiled. Subsequently, a duplicate copy of the file, while the police keep the original, would be sent to the Ministry of Justice for the purpose of rendering a legal advice.

E

EASEMENT – It simply connotes a legal right to use another person's portion of land as a means of access to one's own property or to lay sewage or water pipes through another's land. This is usually done with a spirit of good neighbourliness in order to promote everyone's enjoyment of his property, even though it is a right which may be enforced in a court of law, if necessary.

EDICT – It is a law made by a state military administrator for the purpose of governing a state. This was prevalent in all the states of the federation before the advent of the democratic era.

EJUSDEM GENERIS – It is a principle of interpreting statutes which states that a general word should be interpreted in the context of specific words used in the same legislation. For example, a clause in a tenancy agreement permitting tenants to rear only a particular class of animals reads in part this way "… tenants can rear goats, fowls, ducks, dogs and other animals." This rule will not permit any tenant to bring a baby crocodile into the premises while relying on the above clause. "Other animals" constitutes a general word which must be interpreted restrictively to mean domestic animals like the particular ones mentioned.

ELEMENTS OF A CRIME - There are things that the prosecution needs to prove in a criminal case in order to attain a proof beyond reasonable doubt as required by law. Each offence has its elements. For example, in a case of rape, the following must be proved: (a) that a suspect has carnal knowledge of a woman or girl without her consent; and (b) that there is penetration even if it is slight.

ENCUMBRANCE – It means any right or interest in land which constitutes a challenge to the right of another person over the same land. For example, if a landlord decides to sell his house despite the fact that there are tenants in the house whose tenancy has not expired, whoever buys such house cannot lay absolute claim of ownership over the property without recognising the right of those tenants as well. The house can be said to have been sold subject to *encumbrance*.

ENROLMENT OF ORDER/JUDGEMENT- It is an official summary of a court ruling or judgement prepared and issued to parties in a case until the full version is available. This summary is to be used temporarily before the full judgement is ready.

ESQUIRE - Basically, it means a gentleman. But its use as a suffix to names is dominated by lawyers. In fact, in the U.S., a lawyer's name seems incomplete without it. It is used by American male and female attorneys. In the U.K., it is taken simply to mean a gentleman. The British lawyers are also fond of using it as a suffix to their names. In Nigeria, on the other hand, it is mostly used by male lawyers.

EQUITY - It is a system of law which, like the Common Law, has its origin in England. This system came after the Common Law in order to provide more reliefs than those provided by the Common Law and also to make access to justice easier for people. Some of the guiding principles of this system are *"equity will not suffer a wrong to be without a remedy", "equity aids the vigilant, not the indolent (i.e. those who slumber over their rights)", "equity will not allow a trust to fail for want of a trustee", "equity will not allow a statute to be used as a cloak for fraud", "he who comes to equity must come with clean hands", "equity delights in equality"* and *"he who seeks equity must do equity"*. These principles are popularly known as **MAXIMS OF EQUITY**.

ESTATE PLANNING – It is an arrangement which a person makes concerning his property so as to ensure that the property gets into the hands of one's desired heirs upon the owner's death. *Estate planning* may take different forms e.g. will, trust and living will.

ESTOPPEL - It is a principle of law which prevents a person from going back on his words, actions or positions simply because a liability has arisen. In other words, it holds people bound by their previous actions or promises. For example, a person who has previously created an impression that another person has his authority to act on his behalf would not be allowed to deny the authority given to that person, if a third party sustains some injury by relying on the impression which that person has already created. He is a principal and he is bound by the actions of his agent if carried out within the scope of his authority.

ET NON ALIQUID FACERE EX NIHILO - It means "nothing can stand on nothing".

EX-ABUNDANTI CAUTELA – it means "out of abundant caution". This explains why lawyers use many words where few may be enough because it is believed that it is better to use as many words as possible so as not to leave any room for guess concerning what is being expressed.

EXAMINATION-IN-CHIEF – It is a process by which a party or witnesses give evidence in support of a case.

EXCLUSIVE JURISDICTION – A court is said to have exclusive jurisdiction if it is the only court empowered by law to handle a particular matter or some matters. For example, the National Industrial Court is the court with *exclusive jurisdiction* on any matter having to do with disputes between employees and employers or a matter that has to do with conditions of service of workers.

EX-CONVICT - This is an accused person who has been tried and found guilty and has even served his punishment. A convicted person, having served the jail term, remains an *ex-convict* for life, unless he is later granted pardon.

EX DEBITO JUSTITIAE – It means what a person is entitled to as of right. Usage - *"Workers whose salaries have been withheld without justification are **ex debito justatiae** entitled to be paid with no further delay."*

EXECUTIVE DIRECTOR – This is an officer of a company who is actively involved in day to day management of such company.

EXEMPTION CLAUSES - These are terms in contracts which are meant to enable the party inserting them escape from being held responsible for loss suffered by the other party. Such phrases as *"Cars are parked at owner's risk"*, *"Luggage are kept at owner's risk"* e.t.c are all examples of *exemption clauses* as they are commonly seen in public places. Some terms limiting the liability of an aircraft company to certain weight of passengers' loads are also examples of these clauses. (Compare: **DISCLAIMER**).

EX FACIE CURAE – It means "outside." A contempt of court may be committed ex facie. This is a contempt of court committed through disobedience to a court of order. (Compare: **IN FACIE CURAE**). It is termed civil contempt.

EX GRATIA – It is a payment made out of moral obligation not because of legal right e.g. additional money given to non-striking workers.

EXHIBIT – This is a piece of evidence used in court which must be a physical object. It may be a document, gun, money, goat, human head etc.

EX OFFICIO – It means "by right of office." Usage - *"All past presidents of ASUU are **ex officio** members of the current executive council."*

EX PARTE (INTERIM ORDER) – It is an order of court whose lifespan is 14 days unless extended. It is usually brought without involving the other party. (Compare: **MOTION ON NOTICE**).

EXPATRIATE QUOTA – This is a permit issued by the Ministry of Internal Affairs which authorizes a Nigerian company to employ foreign workers. This permit is not granted indiscriminately; it is usually restricted to specific job positions and the duration of such employment will be specified in the permit.

EXPRESSIO UNIUS EST EXCLUSIO ALTERIUS – It means "the express mention of one thing is the exclusion of another". This Latin expression is normally employed by courts to guide them in the course of interpreting laws, wills, contracts and other legal documents in order to ensure that something not intended by a document is not read into it.

EXPERT WITNESS – This is a specialist in any field invited to a court for the purpose of giving evidence on matters connected to his field. A pathologist may be invited (summoned) in a case of murder to give evidence as to the cause of death of the deceased.

EXTANT LAW - It means an old law which is still in use.

EX TURPI CAUSA NON ORITUR ACTIO – This simply means that nobody is entitled to a remedy in law if the wrong suffered arises from his own illegal act.

F

FACT – It represents the totality of events which forms the basis of a case. For instance, in a case of recovery of debt filed by **A** against **B**, the story of how **B** becomes indebted to **A** and of what transpires between both of them is the fact of the case on the side of **A**. On the side of **B**, **B** may either admit his indebtedness or deny it. If **B** denies, then a narration of the story of his denial forms the fact of his own side of the dispute. So, when evidence is given in a case, it is given to prove the *fact* of the individual's case.

FACT IN ISSUE - This is closely related to "fact" which has been explained above but *fact in issue* is narrower in scope than fact itself. For example, in a divorce petition filed by **Mr. A** against **Mrs. A**, if the latter is also ready and willing that their marriage be dissolved by the court but she is only contesting the property acquired during their marriage with **Mr. A**, then the contention over the property is deemed as the *fact in issue* or, to be put differently, as the fact in dispute between **Mr. A** and **Mrs. A**. The court may forthwith give judgement dissolving their marriage, while it goes into trial to take evidence on the issue of property, whether to decide that the property be shared by both parties or that it belongs solely to one of them.

FAIR HEARING (or **FAIR TRIAL**) – This is said to take place once the rules encapsulated by AUDI ALTERAM PARTEM and NEMO JUDEX IN CAUSA SUA have been complied with. The two Latin words have been explained in this part.

FAIT ACCOMPLI – This term means a completed act. It is normally used to denote a state of things which is beyond remedy. The term may be illustrated by what happened in an old case[8]. It happened that an accused person had been convicted by both the High Court and the Court of Appeal and sentenced to death. He subsequently appealed to the Supreme Court and this Court acquitted him but before the judgement was delivered, the Oyo State government then had carried out the death sentence. So it can be said that a *fait accompli* had been foisted on the decision of the Supreme Court.

FAMILY LAND/PROPERTY – This refers to a parcel of property jointly owned by all members of a particular family. Once property is jointly owned by members of a family, no single member can sell such property without the concurrence of all other family members or head of the family.

FELONY – It is a crime which attracts a punishment of not less than three years imprisonment and which is usually tried by a court not lower than a high court e.g. rape and murder. However, magistrate court may try few felonious cases.

---

[8]. See, Bello v. Attorney-General, Oyo State (1986) 5 NWLR Pt. 45, 825.

FIAT - It is an order of court commanding the doing of a particular act.

FIAT JUSTITIA RUAT CAELUM - It means that justice must be done even if heaven will fall. In other words, it is a doctrine which enjoins courts to do justice in every case without fear or favour.

FIDUCIARY RELATIONSHIP – it is a relationship between two or more persons which is based on mutual trust and good faith. Relationships between principal/agent, the insurer/the insured, partners in a partnership business, etc, are examples of *fiduciary relationships*. Parties in *fiduciary relationships* owe themselves certain duties called fiduciary duties. Some of these duties are full disclosure among themselves, not to make secret profit and keeping of confidential information.

FIERI FACIAS (shortened as **FI.FA** and is also known as **WRIT OF EXECUTION**) – It is a court order directing an official of court to carry out a judgment. It may come in form of removing a debtor's (otherwise known as a judgement debtor) property to the court's premises so as to sell it (i.e. auction) in order to settle his debt to the judgment creditor. (Compare: **WRIT OF POSSESSION**).

FINAL JUDGEMENT – This represents a judgment entered in a case which captures all the issues involved in a case. Any party who is displeased with the judgement of the court at this stage may have to appeal to a higher court.

FINES – It is a form of punishment which may be imposed by a court on an accused person who has been tried and found guilty of a crime. It usually requires a convict to pay a specified sum of money into the government coffers. Some offences have alternative punishments which may require a convict to either pay *fine* or go to jail but most serious offences such as manslaughter do not have the option of *fine*.

FORCE MAJEUR - It is a situation that is beyond human control e.g. earthquake, outbreak of war etc. This kind of situations is recognized by law as capable of rendering the performance of a contract impossible in which case a breach of contract would not be ascribed to the fault of any party. Some contract agreements take into consideration what effect a situation of *force majeur*, where it happens, will have on the outstanding obligations of the parties. This is a good practice.

FORECLOSURE - It is a situation where a mortgagor loses his mortgaged property to a mortgagee as a result of the failure of the former to keep to the terms of repaying the sum of money involved in the mortgaged agreement. (For more details, see **MORTGAGE**).

FORFEITURE – It is an order that may be made in a criminal case which retrieves (i.e. confiscates) products of criminal activity or some portion of items stolen e.g. money from an accused person who has been tried and found guilty. This is usually done in corruption and financial crime cases. This order of *forfeiture* may be made in addition to other punishments such as imprisonment. However, in some civil cases, this order may be made and in such situations, it will not be seen as a punishment. This may occur where a borrower (mortgagor) secures a loan taken by him with his property and upon failure to pay the loan as and when due, the mortgagee may apply to court for forfeiture of the mortgagor's collateral security.

FORUM NON CONVENIENS - This refers to a situation where a court, though it has jurisdiction, would not entertain a matter simply because the location of that court would not be convenient for the other party being sued to attend. For instance, a case filed in Federal High Court, Abuja where all the parties as well as their potential witnesses reside in Oyo State may warrant the Abuja court to decline jurisdiction for the inconvenience that its assumption of jurisdiction would inflict on all concerned. The court's position would be much more reinforced if the root cause of the case also originates from Oyo State.

FORUM SHOPPING - This occurs where a plaintiff appears unsure as to the appropriate court to institute his matter and he is as a result "gambling" by trying his luck in different courts in order to arrive at the appropriate court. Courts usually frown at this practice.

"FROM THE BAR" - When a lawyer says "I am speaking from the Bar", what he is saying is that "I am speaking the whole truth." Once a lawyer says he is speaking from the Bar, it means whatever he says in that regard should be taken as if he is under oath in which case, he has to speak the truth and the court is expected to act on what he says. Also, a lawyer may tender a document "from the Bar", which means the document has to be received by the court and be acted upon as if it is being tendered by a witness given evidence under oath.

FRONT-LOADING PROCESS - It is a system which requires a party filing an action in court to make all his papers (documents) available at once so as ensure a speedy trial of the case. For instance, a plaintiff is required to commence his suit by filing the following documents at once: writ of summons, statement of claim, list of witnesses, witnesses' statements on oath, list of documents and photocopies of all the documents already listed.

FULL COURT – This is a court that has a total number of its judges sitting over a matter. For example, the Supreme Court may sit with a panel of 5 or 7 justices depending on the nature of suits they are dealing with but 7 justices are usually considered as its *full court*. The law requires 5 justices to deal with some matters and 7 justices for some others.

FUNCTUS OFFICIO – It means that once a court has given its ruling or judgment over a matter, the same court cannot reverse itself or revisit that case again. It takes only a higher court to reverse such decision on appeal.

FUNDAMENTAL DEFECT – A case is said to have a *fundamental defect*, if, for instance, its processes are not served on the other party.

Assume a case is started and all the court papers are not served on the person sued, whether judgement has been given or not, the case is fundamentally defective. Any case that is infested with a *fundamental defect* is bound to fail. Some other instances of *fundamental defect* are failure to pay the appropriate filing fees, to file a matter in State **A**'s court instead of State **B** etc.

FURTHER HEARING – This is a case in which witnesses have started giving evidence or which is already in the course of being determined by the court. All the preliminaries of court actions must have been concluded at this stage and the court has started attending to it in its bid to get the case determined.

G

GALLERY – It is the area where people watching a court session sit. It may consist of litigants, their witnesses and other members of the public.

GARNISHEE PROCEEDINGS/ORDER – it is basically an application taken at the instance of a judgement creditor against a judgement debtor so as to ensure that the judgement debtor's money is attached wherever it may be found e.g. money in his bank account or money owed him by a third party. This is done by a judgement creditor so that there will be money to offset the judgement debtor's indebtedness to him.

GAVEL – It is a hammer-like object used in courts, usually by the presiding judge, to command orderliness at any stage of a court session. It may also be used to announce the close of a court sitting.

GAZETTE - It is a government publication issued from time to time so as to keep members of the public informed in relation to government activities. Any information published in a gazette is a notice to the whole world.

GOING CONCERN – It simply means a company which is functioning at the present and whose condition gives hope for continuous operations without threat of liquidation in the future, say within 12 months.

GOLDEN RULE – This is a rule of interpretation of statutes which permits judges to interpret laws in a manner that the intentions of the lawmakers would be served and justice be done.

GOVERNOR'S CONSENT – This is the approval that must be given by a governor of a state or his delegate in any transaction that has to do with the transfer of ownership or other interest over land or landed property in order to make the transaction valid at law. Examples of documents transferring interests in land that require the *Governor's consent* are mortgage, procurement of certificate of occupancy, deed of assignment etc.

GRATIS – It means something received free of charge or out of favour. (Compare: **PRO-BONO**)

GRAVAMEN – It simply means "the basis." Usage – *"The gravamen of my argument is that it is contrary to the Nigerian constitution to discriminate against any Nigerian on the basis of his state of origin."*

GROSS MISCONDUCT – This word does not seem to have precise meaning nor is there an exhaustive list of acts which constitute *gross misconduct*. However, certain acts over time have been regarded as *gross misconduct* when they are committed by an employee in his employment. Examples of acts which may amount to *gross misconduct* include drunkenness, habitual late-coming, sexual harassment, incompetence, laziness, and so on. An employee who commits any of these may be dismissed even without notice. Apart from employment matters, the issue of gross misconduct may also arise in impeachment proceedings where executive heads such as the President, Vice-President, governors, deputy-governors or local government chairmen may be relieved of their positions on account of acts of gross misconduct.

GRUNDNORM – This term is commonly used to describe a country's constitution which simply means that the constitution is the basic and the highest law of the land and no law must be contrary to its provisions.

GUARANTEESHIP (also known as **GUARANTY**) - It is a contract where a person called guarantor promises or undertakes to pay another's debt where the debtor fails to pay his debt at the agreed time. However, for this kind of contract to be binding on a guarantor, it must have been made in writing. An oral promise or undertaking will not bind a guarantor. (For more details, see **UNENFORCEABLE CONTRACTS**).

GUARDIAN AD LITEM – This is an adult (a special guardian) who stands in position of an infant in relation to a court action instituted against the infant. His duty is to stand for the infant as if the case is against his person. In other words, a *guardian ad litem* defends an action which is really against an infant.

H

HABEAS CORPUS – It is a legal process which requires a person in custody to be produced in court for the purpose of deciding whether to release him or keep him further in detention.

HEARING – It is a stage at which a case is ripe to be heard by a court when evidence will be taken as all necessary court papers in respect of the case must have been filed.

HEARING NOTICE - It is a notice served on parties to a case or their lawyers (where they are represented by lawyers) in order to intimate them about the date their case is coming up in court and what it is being slated for.

HEARSAY EVIDENCE – It is a piece of evidence that does not originate from a witness' personal experience. It is more or less a rendition of an account obtained from a person who is not a witness before the court. In common language, it may be referred to as third or second-hand information. *Hearsay evidence* is generally not allowed in court.

HIRE PURCHASE - It is a business arrangement where one party otherwise known as the owner gives goods to another called the hirer whereby the latter will be making some periodical payment (technically known as instalments) to the former until the full cost of the goods is off-set. Upon the full payment of the purchase price, the ownership of the goods would be transferred to the hirer. Until the transfer of ownership takes place, the hirer is not the owner and therefore, he cannot handle the goods as if it belongs to him.

HIRER - This is a person who is given custody of goods by its owner until the time when the former (i.e. the *hirer*) would complete the payment of instalments. Once a *hirer* completes the instalmental payments, he becomes the owner and can do whatever thing he likes with the goods.

HOLDING BRIEF - It is a kind of arrangement between two lawyers where one lawyer is standing in temporarily for the other lawyer in a case until the other lawyer is available to continue with the handling of his case personally.

HOLDING CHARGE (sometimes spelt as "**HOLDEN**") - It is a practice where people suspected to have committed some crimes are kept in custody by the order of court while police investigation is still on-going. This practice has been condemned by courts because it violates individuals' right to personal liberty.

HOSTILE WITNESS – This is a person invited by a party in a case in order to testify in favour of the party who has called him but whose evidence tends to be heading against the interest of the party that calls him.

I

IDENTIFICATION PARADE – It is a queue of a number of suspects arranged by the police in which a victim of a crime is invited to identify the perpetrator of the crime against him. This is done in order to be sure that a suspect is indeed the offender through the proper identification of the latter by the victim.

IGNORANTIA JURIS NON EXCUSAT – It simply means "ignorance of law is not an excuse." The implication of this legal principle is that it is not a defence for anyone who commits a crime or breaches his obligation under a contract to say that he does not know that what he does is against the law.

IGNORANTIA LEGIS NEMINEM EXCUSAT - It means "ignorance of fact may excuse but not ignorance of law".

ILLEGAL CONTRACT – This is a contract that violates the law and which cannot be enforced. For instance, if a man hires another person to impersonate his son in order to write an examination on behalf of the son and the hired man (i.e. mercenary) collects money but fails to carry out the assignment; there is nothing that the other man can do because this is a contract for the commission of an offence and it is illegal.

IMMUNITY - It is a protection from law suits granted to certain political office-holders in Nigeria. These political office-holders are governors, deputy-governors, president and vice-president. While no legal action can be brought against these persons in their personal capacity during their terms of office, they are not prevented from initiating actions in courts against other people if they have to.

IMPEACHMENT - It is a procedure laid down by the constitution and some other laws by which certain persons holding executive offices such as the president, governors, local government chairmen and others may be removed from office before the expiration of their tenure. It is a form of built-in checks which enables law-makers to curtail executive excesses.

INCORPORATION – It is a process by which a company is registered in accordance with the laid down rules and regulations. Once a company is incorporated with the Certificate of Incorporation issued, it becomes a legal entity. (See, **LEGAL ENTITY**).

INDICTABLE OFFENCE – It means a serious offence for which punishment exceeds two years' imprisonment e.g. stealing.

INDICTMENT – It refers to a state of finding a person liable to be charged with a crime.

IN FACIE CURAE - This refers to acts of disrespect committed in the face of court, amounting to contempt of court e.g. engaging in side talks while a court session is on-going or abusing a judge to his face. Any of these acts is regarded as contempt *in facie curae* which is punishable outright.

INFERIOR COURT OF NO RECORD - This encompasses all courts below the status of a high court because in such courts, the application of the principle of judicial precedent is limited or almost absent. Unlike superior courts whose judgments are found in law reports, the judgements of these courts are not reported; hence, they cannot be used as precedents. Again, in courts such as customary and Sharia courts, decisions of superior courts are not being used as precedent.

INJUNCTION – It is an order of court which seeks to restrain a party or parties from the doing of an act. It may also compel the doing of an act e.g. an order of mandamus (also known as mandatory injunction).

INJURIA SINE DAMNO - This means "legal injury without damage". This refers to a situation where an action, regarded at law as a legal wrong, done by a person (say, a defendant) is deemed to constitute a legal injury even if a plaintiff has not suffered any tangible or physical injury. For instance, if a defamatory statement is written concerning another person, the writer of such defamatory writing is liable to pay damages to the plaintiff, even though the latter has not suffered any injury as a result of the defamation. This is what is meant by saying that libel is *actionable per se.*

IN LIMINE - It means "at the outset". It is a kind of application made in court in order to truncate a suit from the beginning.

IN LOCO PARENTIS – It means "in the place of a parent". It refers to a person who stands in place of parent to another.

INNER BAR - It is used to qualify a body of Senior Advocates of Nigeria. It also means the front-row in court which is normally reserved for or occupied by Senior Advocates of Nigeria whenever some or one of them is in court. (Compare: **OUTER BAR**).

IN PARI DELICTO – It means "in equal fault." For instance, if one person engages another person to write his examination for him, both parties can be said to be blameworthy and neither may enforce the contract.

IN PARI MATERIA – It means "upon the same matter or subject." Usage – *"The evidence the witness gave in court was in pari materia with the statement he made at the police station."*

INQUISITORIAL SYSTEM – This is a system of criminal law where a judge is also the one prosecuting a suspect. The judge cannot be said to be unbiased in this kind of system, though the system allows the suspect to have a lawyer defending him.

INSIDER TRADING – It is a kind of dealings in company shares by persons who, by their official positions, have access to privileged information which information they use for their own advantage at the expense of those who deal with them. For example, this may occur where some management staff of a company prompt some shareholders to dispose of their shares because of confidential information at their disposal which forecasts likely appreciation in the values of shares. In this case, they may buy shares at cheap prices while they hope to sell at higher prices when the forecast materialises.

INSOLVENCY - It is a state (or condition) in which a person or company is unable to meet his or its financial obligations as they arise or unable to pay debts. (Compare: **BANKRUPTCY**).

INTENTION TO CREATE LEGAL RELATIONS – This is one of the elements required in a contract. This refers to the state of mind of parties to a contract as to whether they wish to be bound by the agreement they are making or not. They may not express their wish clearly but the court can draw inference from their relationship and what they say or write. For instance, a husband gives his wife some money for her special needs and promises to give her more on a continuous basis but later reneges[9]. The wife files an action in court in order to compel the husband to keep his promise and the court decides that the husband does not intend to be bound by his promise and hence the action fails. Lack of intention to create a contract is usually presumed by courts in certain relationships e.g. husband/wife, parents/children, friends and other family or social relations. However, persons having close relations may expressly state their wish to be bound in order to escape the application of the presumption of courts.

INTER ALIA – It means "among others." Usage – *"Corruption, inept leadership, disunity, are factors, inter alia, that are responsible for Nigeria's underdevelopment."*

---

[9]. Balfour v. Balfour, supra.

INTERLOCUTORY APPLICATION/INJUNCTION – It is a kind of application made in court for the purpose of obtaining a temporary order until a final judgement is given in respect of the main case (See, **SUBSTANTIVE CASE & FINAL JUDGEMENT**).

INTER PARTES – It simply means "between the parties." This plays out when an application is made to be served on the other party to a case. (Contrast: **EX PARTE**).

INTER VIVOS – It is a gift made by a person in his lifetime as opposed to gifts made through a will which take effect after the giver's death.

INTESTACY – This is a state of a person dying without having a valid will.

INTRA VIRES – It means acting within the scope of one's authority.

INVITATION TO TREAT – It means a preliminary step which may lead to the making of an offer. For example, goods displayed in supermarkets constitute an *invitation to treat* and it is a customer that picks them and is ready to pay who is making an offer which, if accepted, creates a contract.

IPSISSIMA VERBA – It means "word for word." Usage – *"He repeated what he wrote in his application letter **ipsissima verba**."*

IPSO FACTO - It means "by the fact itself."

IRREGULARITY – It is a minor defect in a party's case which the other party may not be able to oppose again in the suit if he does not do so immediately he becomes aware of the defect. For example, if a court paper is served on **House A** instead of **House B**, but where a party in **House B** becomes aware of the service and appears in court without complaining while he also reacts by filing his own papers, he cannot subsequently complain about the wrong service. The issue of wrong service will be treated as mere *irregularity* which cannot nullify a case. (Contrast: **FUNDAMENTAL DEFECT**).

J

JACTITATION OF MARRIAGE - It is a claim made by a person to be married to another person when in actual fact there is no marriage between the two. This is usually done by the person making the claim in order to boost his own prestige at the expense of another's reputation.

JOINDER OF PARTIES – When a suit is filed in court, all persons affected by that suit should be made parties to it. So anybody left out in the suit may be added as the case progresses through a process called *joinder of parties*.

JOINTLY AND SEVERALLY (better known as **JOINTLY AND SEVERALLY LIABLE**) - It is one of the ways by which a plaintiff suing more than one defendant in a case may make his claims against all of them. The implication of this is that if a sum of money is awarded in favour of the plaintiff, he is at liberty to get the full judgement money paid by all or by any of the defendants. Where the plaintiff opts to pursue one defendant and gets paid by such defendant, it remains the internal issue of the defendants to sort out how the money solely paid by one is contributed by others.

JOINTLY LIABLE - It means that two or more persons have the same measure of liability to another person. For example, if an action is taken against some persons where a claim of joint liability is made, what this means is that even if one of them is dead, the liability passes jointly to other living persons and the claim can be pursued against one or all of them. Invariably, any or all of them can settle the liability. (Compare: **JOINTLY AND SEVERALLY LIABLE**).

JOINT TENANCY – It means property collectively owned by some people which does not belong to any of the co-owners. The property is not shared; so no portion can be said to belong to any of them. It cannot be sold or transferred by one or some of the co-owners without the agreement of all. Where one of the owners dies, the property passes to the living co-owners and not to the heirs of the dead co-owner.

JOINT VENTURE – It is a business arrangement which involves two or more companies when both are entering a partnership relationship in order to execute a particular project or for a long time business relationship. The rights and responsibilities of parties in this kind of relationship are usually spelt out in a Joint Venture Agreement.

JUDGMENT DEBT – It is a court decision commanding a party who has been found to be indebted to another party to pay a specific sum of money to the party being owed.

JUDICIAL NOTICE - It is a principle which states that the Nigerian law and some phenomenal events need not be proved before local (Nigerian) courts because it is expected of judges and magistrates to keep abreast of these laws and happenings. For example, it is not necessary to give evidence to establish that public offices do not open on Christmas Day or that October 1st is a public holiday in the country. It is presumed that Nigerian courts have taken judicial notice of the country's laws and certain notorious events. However, the courts are not expected to take judicial notice of other countries' laws or events that are peculiar to such countries. Therefore, an expert may need to give evidence in order to prove the existence of a particular principle of law, for example, in China or certain events there whenever such occasions arise before a Nigerian court.

JUDICIAL REVIEW – It is a process by which higher courts e.g. High Court reviews actions or decisions of lower courts, executive and legislative bodies in order to determine whether they comply with constitutional principles or not. Such decisions or actions may be set aside if they fail to so comply with those principles. Certiorari and mandamus are examples of judicial review procedures.

JUDICIAL SEPARATION - It is a court order which merely permits a couple to live apart for a specified length of time. So, *judicial separation* does not dissolve a marriage. The parties remain married except that they are no longer living together as couple.

JUMP BAIL – A suspect who is on bail and who fails to attend court on a day when his matter comes up in court is said to have *jumped bail*. If a suspect *jumps bail*, some consequences may follow. A bench warrant may be issued for his re-arrest and if he is re-arrested, it is most likely that he would return to prison. However, if he is nowhere to be found, whoever stands as his surety would be arrested and he would have to lose the bond. (See, **BAIL BOND** and **BENCH WARRANT** above).

JURAT – It is a clause inserted into a document which contains wordings to show that the contents of such document have been read and interpreted to the understanding of one of the parties/signatories to the document who does not understand the language in which the document is written. A document written in English language may contain a *jurat* to show that it has been interpreted in Yoruba language to a signatory to that document. A *jurat* must be included in every document where an illiterate or a blind person is a party (a signatory).

JURISDICTION – It simply connotes the scope of authority or power of a court. In other words, it refers to the nature of matters that a court can handle. For instance, a suit to dissolve a marriage celebrated under the English Law (i.e the Marriage Act) can only be handled by a state high court.

JURY – It is a body of people, usually not lawyers, who are charged with the responsibility of listening to witnesses in a case and giving their decision on the basis of findings they make through the evidence submitted to them. In Nigeria, the *jury* system is not in use.

JUSTICE OF THE PEACE - (usually shortened as JP). This is a person who has been appointed or a person who becomes a *Justice of the Peace* on account of his office (e.g. a magistrate) to exercise certain powers. A *Justice of the Peace* can sign warrant of arrest. An applicant for the office of a *Justice of the Peace* may not be a lawyer.

JUSTICIABILITY – It refers to claims that can be entertained in courts given the position of law. For example, all the provisions relating to the fundamental rights in the Constitution can form the basis of a legal action but the same cannot be said of some other sections in the same constitution.

JUVENILE COURT - It is a special court established to try cases involving children under the age of 18. Cases tried in this court are usually criminal. The court is not open to the public which is meant to shield the identity of the child offender from public ridicule. Even if a child commits a capital offence, death sentence will not be passed on him.

L

LACHES & ACQUIESCENCE – This term is normally used to describe a situation where a person neglects to enforce his right. For example, an owner of a plot of land who keeps aloof while another person moves to his land and takes it over may lose the land to such other person. This is most likely if he does not challenge the person over a length of time in which case it may be said that *laches and acquiescence* has set in.

LACUNA (plural is **LACUNAE**) – It simply means a gap in the law. It is used to refer to an issue which is not covered by law.

LAST IN, FIRST OUT (shortened as **LIFO**) - It is a selection method usually used by employers to determine employees that are to be laid off as a result of redundancy. It means that employees who have been in an employment for the shortest period of time would be relieved of their jobs first.

LAW – It means a statute made by a state house of assembly e.g. Oyo State Signage and Advertisement Law, 2013.

LAW AS AN ASS - The phrase is normally used to condemn rigid and strict application of legal rules. For example, in law, ignorance of law is not an excuse but should a stark illiterate person be prevented from raising a defence of lack of knowledge of law as much as a well-educated fellow? That is the law; whether educated or not, nobody is allowed to plead ignorance of law as a defence. Again, law, in most places, sees marriage as a contract between two people but under the Californian law in the U.S, a human being is legally permitted to marry an animal. How can an animal give its consent to a marriage? Yet under that state's law that is the law, no matter how it runs contrary to common-sense. The phrase (i.e. the law is an ass) was popularised by Charles Dickens in his novel *Oliver Twist* published in 1838.

LEAD JUDGEMENT – If a court is presided over by a judge, whatever judgement given by the court is the judgement of the court as far as that matter is concerned. However, it is a slightly different story where a court is presided over by 5 or 3 justices as is the case in the Supreme Court and the Court of Appeal respectively. In any of these courts (i.e. the Supreme Court and the Court of Appeal) a judgement is said to be the *lead judgement* if it represents the unanimous position of a majority of the justices or all of them in respect of a particular case. (See, **CONCURRING JUDGEMENT** and **DISSENTING JUDGEMENT**).

LEADING QUESTION – It is a question that is suggestive of the expected answer. This kind of questions is not allowed under examination-in-chief. An example of a *leading question* may come in this way – "Are you not a trained accountant?" This question is unacceptable unless it is a build up question to a previous one which has already established the fact that the witness is a trained accountant.

LEASE – It is an agreement that gives rise to a relationship of landlord and tenant. Parties to a lease agreement are usually called lessor and lessee. Unlike the regular tenancy agreement, the duration of a *lease* agreement starts from 3 years to a maximum of 99 years.

LEGAL ADVICE – This is a piece of legal opinion rendered by a lawyer in respect of a particular legal problem so as to proffer legal solution to the problem. *Legal advice* may also be used in another sense. It may be used to describe an opinion rendered by the Department of Public Prosecution in a Ministry of Justice which states whether a suspect or suspects should be or should not be charged for an alleged crime or whether a suspect should be charged for an offence different from the one alleged by the police through their investigation (this is commonly referred to as **D.P.P'S ADVICE**).

LEGAL ENTITY – It means a person with legal rights and duties e.g. a company. Every registered company is a *legal entity* because it has capacity, like a human being, to sue and be sued in its own name.

LEGISLATIVE LIST – The Nigerian Constitution provides for subject-matters that each level of governments is empowered to handle. These subject-matters are categorized into two and the two categories are formally known as **EXCLUSIVE LEGISLATIVE LIST** and **CONCURRENT LEGISLATIVE LIST**. Exclusive Legislative List contains a long list of matters that could only be legislated on by the National Assembly, while those matters found in the Concurrent Legislative List are for both the National Assembly and each State House of Assembly to handle. Some of the matters on the Exclusive List are, defence, exchange control, external affairs, extradition, currency, police and security services.etc. Concurrent List, on the other hand, deals with matters such as electoral law, electric power, scientific and technological research, etc. People have also coined a third list tagged as RESIDUAL LIST. However, this list is not provided for by the Nigerian Constitution. The Residual List is taken to encompass all matters which are not specifically mentioned in the first two lists discussed above.

LESSEE – This is a person who has rented an apartment or premises for a length of time not less than 3 years.

LESSOR – This is a person who has let out his property to another person called lessee for a period not less than 3 years.

LETTERS OF ADMINISTRATION – It is a document issued by a court of law which appoints some people as administrators and gives them power to distribute the property of a person who dies intestate (i.e. without a Will) among his dependants.

LEX NON COGIT IMPOSSIBILIA – It means *"the law does not compel the doing of impossibilities."*

LEX SITUS – This refers to the law of the place where a parcel of land or landed property (e.g. houses) situates.

LIEN – This is a claim that one person has over another person's goods or property, especially if the goods are in the custody of the person who is entitled to such claim. For example, a refrigerator repairer may claim a *lien* over a refrigerator repaired by him, if the owner owes some outstanding balance. The repairer may decide to exercise his right of *lien* by holding on to the refrigerator until his money is paid. However, the repairer does not have the right to sell the refrigerator so as to recover his money without a court order.

LIFTING THE VEIL OF INCORPORATION – It is a process by which a court of law may have to hold persons running a company personally responsible instead of seeing the company as a person on its own that should be responsible for its acts. Courts usually remove (*lift the veil of incorporation*) this legal toga of a company's separate entity, if it is detected that the people running the company are using it as a cloak to cover up their illegal acts.

LIMITED LIABILITY – It is a concept which tends to protect owners of companies by ensuring that where a company fails in its business and its assets cannot meet its liabilities, the owners' losses will not extend beyond whatever they have initially contributed as shares. (Contrast: **PARTNERSHIP**).

LIQUIDATED DAMAGES – This refers to monetary compensation that may be claimed in a suit having to do with contract. An action for monetary compensation is said to be liquidated when the amount being claimed is certain. For example, if a person who is owed some money files an action in court claiming for the recovery of the debt.

LIQUIDATOR – This is a person appointed by a company or a court to wind up the affairs of a company and to distribute its assets, if any, among its creditors.

LIS PENDENS – This is a doctrine which demands that once a dispute over property is before a court, the property cannot be sold or transferred to another person because, if that happens, the buyer does so at his peril.

LITERAL RULE – This is a rule of interpreting statutes which requires courts to interpret words contained in a law in accordance with its dictionary or natural meaning.

LITIGANT – This is a person who is either a plaintiff (claimant) or defendant in a suit.

LITIGATION – It refers to the act of taking an issue or dispute to a court of law for settlement i.e. filing a case in court.

LL.B - It is an abbreviation for **LEGUM BACCALAUREUS** which is a Latin word. In English, it means the Bachelor of Laws. It is a university first degree for those who study law. The use of LL.B is found in England and other countries that take after the English legal system like Nigeria and Ghana. BL, on the other hand, means Barrister at Law which is awarded after a successful completion of the Bar examinations at the Nigerian Law School[10].

LL.M - It is an abbreviation for Legum Magister which, in English, means Master of Laws.

LOCK OUT – It is a situation where an employer prevents his employees from gaining access to their place of work in order to make them accede to his biddings. *Lock out* is a counterpart of strike action.

LOCUS CLASSICUS – This is a case which is the first or one of the first landmark cases decided on a particular principle of law or in which a particular principle of law is extensively considered. For example, **Carlill v. Carbolic Smoke Ball Co. Ltd. (1893)** is considered a *locus classicus* on the principle of unilateral contract.

LOCUS IN QUO – It means the place where an event takes place. It may mean a particular plot of land over which parties in court are suing themselves. On some occasions, a court may have to visit the *locus in quo* in order to verify conflicting claims of parties.

LOCUS STANDI – This means that a party filing an action in court must be personally affected by the circumstances that bring about that action in the first place. Cases are usually struck out where it is established that a party suing does not have any personal interest in the matter. If **A** is owed some money by **B**, **C** cannot have *locus standi* to sue **B** in order to recover the money.

LUCID PERIOD/INTERVAL – This refers to a brief period of normalcy experienced by a drunken or insane person in which any legal or illegal act done at this period by him is said to be binding on

---

[10]. "What Do The Letters LLB Stand For?" http://writehouse.biz/?p=2793 (accessed on 12th February, 2014).

him. For instance, if an insane person enters into a contract during his lucid interval, such contract is binding on him.

M

MAGISTRATE – This is a lawyer appointed as a judicial officer by a state government to adjudicate over minor offences and civil matters which do not involve huge sums of money. A lawyer must have a minimum of 4 years' post-call experience in order to be qualified for appointment, though this differs from state to state.

MAGNA CARTA – It is a Latin word which means "Great Charter" in English. It was one of the earliest documents on human rights. It was a document which tried to place some limit on the powers of the King of England.

MALA FIDE – It means to do something out of bad faith or malice.

MANAGING DIRECTOR – This is a company director considered the most senior among other directors. He provides overall direction to others as well as the company. He is the head of the management team. Traditionally, in the UK, like Nigeria, anybody holding a position of this nature in a company is called managing director, while in the US, such a person is called chief executive officer (CEO).

MANDAMUS – It is a command issued by a superior court to an inferior court or to a public institution requiring it to carry out a duty which it should have performed. It may come in the form of an order to, for example, the police to investigate an influential personality who has been suspected to have committed a crime.

MANSLAUGHTER – It is an unintentional and unlawful killing of a human being. Where a case of *manslaughter* is proved beyond reasonable doubt, it attracts life imprisonment.

MATERIAL EVIDENCE – It is a piece of evidence which is important to prove a case. It also follows that a witness giving *material evidence* is a material witness. For instance, an eye-witness to a criminal incident can be said to be a material witness because he can give credible and *material evidence* in respect of the incident.

MEDIATION – It means an amicable settlement of disputes. It is usually a win-win approach to settlement of disputes for the purpose of maintaining friendly relations among parties.

MEDDLESOME INTERLOPPER - It is used to refer to a person who intrudes into another person's affairs when he is not being invited. In other words, it means a busy-body. Also, where a person files an action in court, when he does not have *locus standi*, he may be described as meddlesome interlopper.

MEETINGS – For a company to attend to its affairs, members and directors may have to come together and discuss. Some of the *meetings* usually held by companies are annual general meeting (AGM), statutory meeting and extra-ordinary meeting.

MEMORANDUM OF APPEARANCE – This is usually the first court paper to be filed by a defendant who intends to defend a suit being filed against him. It contains the name of the case, its assigned case number, the number of the court where the matter is coming up (if the matter has been assigned to a court), the address of the defendant or that of his lawyer, and it will indicate that by the document, an appearance has been entered for the defendant.

MEMORANDUM OF ASSOCIATION - It is a document that regulates the relationship between the company and the outside world. It addresses issues of concern to the outside world such as the name of the company, its official address, the working capital of the company, the type of the company, nature of business and its subscribers. Memorandum and Articles of Association could collectively be regarded as the constitution of a company. However, where there is a conflict between the two, *Memorandum of Association* would prevail.

MEMORANDUM OF UNDERSTANDING (shortened as MoU) - It is a formal agreement between two or more parties which is usually not binding until a valid contract is drawn up and signed by the parties. However, there are occasions when MoU may be binding especially if parties through their use of words show intention to be bound. MoU is commonly used by multinational companies. MoU is known as Letter of Intent in the US.

MENS REA – (also known as "guilty mind" or "criminal intention"). This refers to a state of mind of an accused person (also known as defendant) which has to be established in a criminal charge in order to show that he has intention to commit the alleged offence. So in a criminal trial, it is not enough that a crime has been committed, it is also important to prove that the accused person has the intention to commit the crime. This may be established by giving evidence on the manner he carried out the criminal act. For instance, in a case of murder, it must be proved that the accused person intends to kill or cause serious injury to the person killed. (Contrast: **STRICT LIABILITY OFFENCES**).

MENTION – It means a case which is not ripe yet to take arguments of lawyers or evidence of witnesses. When a case is slated for mention, another date will be taken on which argument or evidence will commence. It should be noted further that matters slated for mention can only proceed to argument or the taking of evidence, if all the parties to the case are ready. However, with the introduction of frontloading system into civil cases in most states of the federation, a situation of listing cases for mention is no more in vogue in this area, while the same cannot be said of criminal matters.

MESNE PROFITS[11] – It is a kind of monetary claim being made against a person who wrongfully occupies a premises or apartment after the expiration of his tenancy. For instance, if a tenant is occupying an apartment after his tenancy has expired, any "rents" that fall due during the period he occupies to the time he gives up possession of the premises is known as *mesne profits* which the landlord may sue to recover.

MISDEMEANOUR – This refers to minor offences for which punishments are below year or small amount of money as fine. Magistrate courts can try such offences summarily. (See, **COURT OF SUMMARY JURISDICTION** above).

MISREPRESENTATIONS – It is a statement, term or anything done in respect of a contract which turns out to be untrue and which has induced another party to the contract to enter into it in the first place. Misrepresentation may be innocent, negligent or fraudulent misrepresentation. *Misrepresentation,* most especially fraudulent misrepresentation, nullifies a contract, if it is successfully proved.

MOCK TRIAL - This is an imitation of court proceedings at which law students argue hypothetical cases for the purpose of preparing themselves for tasks ahead upon becoming full-fledged lawyers. Mock trials represent cases which take place in lower courts such as the Magistrate's Court and High Court. (Compare: **MOOT COURT**).

MODUS OPERANDI – It means method of doing things. It may be used to describe the pattern of operation of a group of people or organisation. Usage - *"An examination of the time and level of destruction left behind as a result of the weekend attack on the shopping complex portrays the **modus operandi** of the most dreaded terrorist organisation in the city."*

---

[11]. For more details, see Debs v. Cenico Ltd. (1986) 3 NWLR Pt. 32, 846 at 853.

MOOT COURT - This is the same as the **MOCK TRIAL** defined above but while mock trial is used for cases taking place before courts of first instance e.g. Magistrate's Court, moot court is used for appeals which arise from decisions given at the stage of mock trials. In other words, moot court is regarded as an appellate court e.g. the Court of Appeal.

MORATORIUM - It is a period of waiting or suspension in the doing of an act. For example, in relation to whether death penalty should be abolished or not in places where it remains a legal form of punishment, a moratorium may be allowed in which no death penalty will be carried out while the debate on its abolition is on-going. It may also be used concerning payment of a debt and in that case, the payment of the debt will be delayed for some time.

MORTGAGE – This is an agreement where the owner of property especially landed property transfers his documents of title over such property to another person in order to serve as a collateral security for a loan obtained by such property owner. Parties to a mortgage agreement are mortgagor and mortgagee.

MOTION EX PARTE – It is an application or paper filed in court in an emergency situation and it does not need to be served on an opponent in a suit. It is normally used to obtain an interim order from a court.

MOTION ON NOTICE – It is an application, as opposed to motion ex parte, which must be served on an opponent in a suit. It must be supported by an affidavit. This may be used to achieve a number of purposes in judicial proceedings e.g. to obtain an interlocutory injunction. (See, **INTERLOCUTORY APPLICATION** above).

MURDER – This is an unlawful and intentional killing of a human being. The punishment is death by hanging.

MUTATIS MUTANDI – It means "things are generally the same except with some changes in terms of details".

N

NECESSARY GOODS – These are goods which are deemed necessary to meet a person's basic needs especially women and people who have not attained contractual age of 21 years. Foods, clothings, shoes, books e.t.c may be regarded as *necessary goods*.

NEGOTIABLE INSTRUMENTS – These are documents designed for making payments in respect of which ownership may be transferred from one person to another until the final payment is made. Examples of *negotiable instruments* are bill of exchange, cheques, promissory notes, treasury bills, banker's draft etc.

NEMO DAT QUOD NON HABET – It means "you cannot give a title that you do not have." A person who does not own a thing cannot sell it except with the express permission of the owner. So where a thief sells a thing he has stolen to another person, the buyer of such thing must give it up to the real owner whenever the latter surfaces.

NEMO JUDEX IN CAUSA SUA – It means "nobody can be a judge in his own case." This principle prohibits a judge or anybody who is in a position to decide another person's fate not to go ahead, if he knows any of the parties or he is personally interested in the matter. For instance, this principle may be violated where a judge presides over a case in which his relation is one of the parties.

NEXT FRIEND – This is a person who represents a plaintiff who cannot represent himself because of his disability e.g. an infant. More often than not, a *next friend* is a relative or someone very close to the plaintiff who does not possess legal capacity to file an action in his own name.

NEXT OF KIN – This is the closest blood relation of another person. The law does not confer any legal right on a *next of kin*. The use of *next of kin* is more of administrative requirement.

NO CASE SUBMISSION – (In common language, it is known as **NO CASE TO ANSWER**). It is an application that is made by a suspect which is meant to terminate the prosecution's case prematurely by asserting that the prosecution has failed to establish a tangible case against the suspect which would warrant him to give evidence in his defence. If a court accedes to this kind of application, then the court would make an order discharging and acquitting the suspect.

NOLLE PROSEQUI – It is the power given to the Attorney-General, whether of a State or of the Federation, to terminate a criminal trial irrespective of the gravity of the offence alleged against a suspect. While it is required that, in exercising this power, the Attorney-General should take into account the effect that such termination may have on the interest of the general public, he cannot be questioned on his exercise of this power.

NON COMPOS MENTIS - It means a person who is not of sound mind or a person not mentally competent to manage his own affairs.

NON EST FACTUM – It means "not my act." It is a kind of defence that may be raised by a person who is trying to escape liability as a result of a document signed by him.

NON-EXECUTIVE DIRECTOR – This is an officer of a company who is not involved in a day-to-day running of the company. His input is limited to the formulation of policy directions for the company. (Contrast: **EXECUTIVE DIRECTOR**).

NON SEQUITUR – It means "it does not follow".

NON-SUIT- It is a judgment given in a situation where neither a plaintiff nor a defendant is able to establish his case to the satisfaction of the court in order to deserve a favourable judgment. Simply put, none of the parties wins the case. The judgement does not, however, preclude a plaintiff from re-filing the same case.

NOTARY PUBLIC – It is a status that can only be attained by a lawyer who must have been qualified as a lawyer for a period of not less than 8 years. The status permits a lawyer to use a special stamp while signing some documents and he can also sign as a commissioner for oaths. In addition, it affords a lawyer opportunity to render certain services which an ordinary legal practitioner cannot and brings him additional incomes.

NOTICE OF APPEAL – It is a court paper (process) used in initiating an appeal in a higher court where a lower court's judgement is being found unfavourable by a party (i.e. the **APPELLANT**) and it is therefore being challenged. *Notice of appeal* is usually filed at the registry of the lower court that gives the judgement being appealed against, though it is headed in the name of the higher court.

NOTICE OF DISCONTINUANCE – This is a paper filed in court especially by a claimant in order to terminate his suit. This is commonly done before parties begin to give evidence in a case. It is also not a kind of application that the other party may oppose because a claimant has the discretion to withdraw an action initiated by him in the first place.

NOVATION – it means the replacement of an old contract with a new one. This may play out where a bank enters into an agreement with another bank so as to off-set a customer's indebtedness to the other bank in order to win the customer over to its own side. What this means is that a new contract now exists between the two banks while the individual customer is no longer a party to it.

NOVUS ACTUS INTERVIENIENS - It means "a break in the chain of causation". It is a form of defence which a defendant may raise in a civil case bordering on torts. For a defendant to be liable in a tortious wrong e.g. negligence, a plaintiff must be able to connect the act of the defendant to his injury and there must not be a break in the chain of this event. For example, assuming a manufacturer of soft drinks is not careful and some of the drinks are contaminated and a consumer takes the contaminated drinks and sustains some injury as a result. If the consumer, instead of seeking for medical treatment, decides to resort to self-medication which rather complicates his condition, the manufacturer may try to dodge liability by asserting that the drugs taken by the consumer has made it impossible to connect the drinks initially taken to the consumer's present predicament.

NUGATORY – This is normally used to depict a situation where a party takes a step which has a negative effect on a matter in court. A step taken by a party which may render whatever decision a court gives useless is considered to be nugatory. (See, **FAIT ACCOMPLI** above).

NULL AND VOID – This phrase is normally used to denote "nothing" or to mean that something cannot have any effect, especially if it is something that is faulty from the beginning. For example, if an administrative body, not being a court of law, determines the fate of persons alleged to have committed some crimes, it can be said that whatever decision made by such administrative body is *null and void*. Only a court of law can try offenders.

O

OATH – It is a declaration made before any person authorised to take solemn declarations which are supposed to be honest and true. It also represents the declaration that is made on a religious book by a witness in court by which he is bound to speak nothing but the truth.

OBITER DICTUM – This is the portion of a court judgement which is more of a side remark made by that court in its judgement. It is regarded as a side remark because it does not deal with the main issue in contention between the parties to a suit. For example, let us assume that what is before the court to determine in respect of a case is the question of rightful person to occupy a vacant throne. Having decided the issue, the court goes further to remark that traditional processes for enthroning community leaders should not be a matter for court intervention. This remark will constitute an *obiter dictum* because it represents the judge's own view and not an opinion based on law which arises from issues in dispute between parties. Such remark is not binding on lower courts even in a related matter.

OBJECTS CLAUSE – It is a portion of a company's memorandum of association which spells out a list of business activities that the company can carry out. A company acts *ultra vires*[12] when it goes outside its objects clause.

OCCUPIER'S LIABILITY - Every owner of premises has a duty of care towards anybody that enters his premises either on invitation or not. If injury occurs to a visitor, the owner is deemed to be liable in damages.

OFFENDER - This word may be used interchangeably with suspect and law-breaker. See, SUSPECT below for details.

OFFER – This is a clear proposal made to another person with an intention to enter into a contract with the other, if he accepts the proposal.

OFFICIAL WITNESS - This is a police officer or any other public servant who has to give evidence in court as different from private individuals.

OUTER BAR - It is used to refer to a body of lawyers who have not become Senior Advocates of Nigeria and as such are not entitled to certain privileges which are only available to the Senior Advocates of Nigeria.

---

[12]. See, below.

OUT OF COURT & OUT OF HEARING - This is an announcement usually made by a court registrar when evidence is about to be given in a case which is an instruction to potential witnesses to go out of court and move to a place away from the court so that they do not hear what evidence is being given. This rule does not, however, apply to a party, whether plaintiff or defendant, in a case. The rule is meant to ensure that witnesses give evidence of what they know and not necessarily repeat what they have heard a previous witness say.

OVERNIGHT CASE - This is used to refer to suspects who are being brought to courts, usually magistrate courts, for the first time from police custody. Applications would be made for their bails, provided that criminal cases against them are within the powers of a magistrate court to grant bails and if the magistrate court cannot release them on bail, then an order would be made to remand them in prison custody until they are properly charged before a court that has jurisdiction to try them. Though, once in a while, the court may order that they be taken back to police custody.

OVERRULING – This is a judgement of a higher court nullifying a previous judgment made by itself in a later case. This may occur where the Supreme Court, for instance, decides to set aside any of its own former judgements. The word "overruling" is also used when a party's point of objection is turned down by a court.

P

PACTA SUNT SERVANDA - The term has two meanings: (1) it means that an agreement must be kept and (2) it means that countries must keep their obligations under treaties. The first relates to the law of contract while the second is a fundamental principle of international law.

PARENT COMPANY (HOLDING COMPANY) - This is a company that has substantial shares in the capital of another company or companies. Those other companies are known as subsidiaries.

PAROL CONTRACT - It means a contract which is wholly verbal.

PAROLE - It is a practice which permits a convicted criminal to be set free from the prison before he completes his jail term. This is usually done where it is seen that a convict has transformed positively and is fit to go back to the society. However, this practice is not in use in Nigeria.

PARRI PASSU - It means "side by side" or "at the same rate." Usage - *"All the company's shares rank **parri passu**."* This means that the company's share, whether preference or ordinary shares have the same rights.

PARTICIPES CRIMINES – This refers to persons who take part in a criminal act. In order words, it means parties to a crime.

PASSING OFF – It is a form of civil wrong which occurs where one person gives his business a name which is the same or closely similar to one which is already in existence and which may, by so doing, mislead customers of the first business name to take the later name for the first. The law protects businesses in this way so that a new-comer into a business will not take undue advantage of the goodwill that an existing business has already established.

PAST CONSIDERATION – It is a form of promise which a party gives in respect of a former contract and which is not valid to sustain a present promise. For instance, if at a road intersection, while you wait for traffic light, somebody walks up to your car and cleans your windscreen without you asking, any promise you make thereafter to pay him for work done is not binding on you. This is because his cleaning of the windscreen constitutes a *past consideration* which cannot sustain your present promise to pay.

PATENT – This is the right of a person who has made an invention which entitles him to the exclusive use of what is invented and to prevent others from having access to the constituents of such invention for a number of years.

PAYEE – This is a person whose name is written on a cheque. In other words, he is the person to take the benefit of the amount of money written on that cheque.

PENDENTE LITE – It means a suit which is still on-going (pending) in court. Parties are supposed to maintain things as they are until a case is decided.

PER CURIAM - It means a decision that is taken by a whole court as distinct from one taken by a particular judge. (Compare: **CORAM**).

PERFECTION OF BRIEF – When a lawyer says "my brief has not been perfected" what this means is that his client has not paid his professional fees. If it happens that a lawyer's brief has not been perfected, he may decide to withdraw his further appearance in such client's case.

PER INCURIAM – This is a court decision that is made in error. The error may arise from the failure of a court to consider an important law before arriving at its decision when it would have arrived at a different decision, if the omission had not occurred.

PERJURY – It is the offence of making a false statement in an affidavit or any false statement made on oath whether in writing or verbally. *Perjury* is a crime and attracts 14 years' imprisonment.

PER SE – It simply means "as it is".

PERSONAL PROPERTY - This refers to all property that is movable e.g. cars, clothings, electronics and so on.

PERSONAL REPRESENTATIVE – This includes executor and administrator. For details, see my book titled, HOW TO WRITE YOUR WILL WITH EASE.

PERSONAL SERVICE – It is more or less a standing rule that court papers filed in commencing a new case must be served on persons being sued directly and not on their representatives. However, if it is impossible to achieve this for whatever reason, an application may be made to a court to allow for an alternative means of effecting service of court papers which is technically known as substituted service. (See, **SUBSTITUTED SERVICE** below)

PERSUASIVE AUTHORITY – This refers to the weight or effect that a case being cited has over a lower court. The judgement of a higher court is said to have *persuasive authority* on a lower court if the judgement is *obiter dictum* and not *ratio decidendi* (the meanings of the two Latin words have been explained elsewhere in this part). Similarly, a judgement of one court may have persuasive effect on another court if the two courts are on the same level of judicial hierarchy e.g. a State High Court and the Federal High Court. A lower court is not bound to follow a judgement that merely has *persuasive authority*.

PICKETING – This is a form of industrial action where workers gather at the entrance of their place of work in order to prevent any worker from working as well as entering the work premises. An imaginary line (popularly called *picketing* line) is deemed to be drawn which no worker must cross.

PIRACY - It may mean a crime of robbing a ship at sea or a crime of copying films, music, computer software and other similar electronic materials for commercial purpose without the authorisation of the owner of such works.

PLAGIARISM – It means a verbatim or a substantial reproduction of another person's writing without acknowledging the author of such writing. *Plagiarism* is an act of intellectual 'stealing'. It is a crime if the original work is protected in accordance with the copyright law.

PLAINT (PRAECIPE) – It is a court paper used in commencing a civil suit in a magistrate court.

PLAINTIFF – See the meaning of claimant.

PLEA – It is the stage at which an accused person is asked in court to respond whether he is guilty or not guilty to an alleged crime that has been read to him. It is this response of the accused person of either "I am guilty" or "I am not guilty" that is called the *plea*. Statements like "I am guilty with reasons" or "I am not guilty with reasons" are not the proper way to express a *plea*. However, in a capital offence, if an accused person pleads "I am guilty", the court has a duty to record "not guilty" for him and he is given an opportunity to go through a full-fledged trial as if he had earlier pleaded not guilty[13].

PLEA BARGAINING[14] – This is a negotiation which takes place between an accused person and the prosecution where the former pleads guilty to a lesser crime, while the latter agrees in turn to drop a more serious crime. This method is usually employed in the trial of financial crime cases by making it part of the negotiation for the accused person to surrender some portion of money which he has embezzled and for which he is being tried. The method is also used to save time and decongest courts.

---

[13]. It should be noted that this rule does not apply to a non-capital offence where a court can pass a sentence on such accused person forthwith.

[14]. This practice has generated a lot of controversies in Nigeria. Some believe that the practice is illegal while some others believe otherwise. Aside from this argument, some also believe that it is a ploy to provide soft-landing for high-profile offenders, while mere "goat-thieves" are sentenced to 14 years or more in prison. A brief response to this opinion is that a court is also bound by law and sentences imposed by courts are determined by whatever punishments prescribed by relevant statutes for respective offences.

PLEADINGS – This is a general term given to such court papers as statement of claim, statement of defence and so on.

PLEDGE – It is a deposit of personal belongings including land as collateral security for the repayment of some debt.

POINT OF LAW – It is an argument which is based purely on what the law says and not facts. Lawyers usually enjoy the prerogative to address courts on the position of law on a particular matter and the opportunity is rarely extended to non-lawyers who are handling their cases by themselves.

POLICE PROSECUTOR - It is used to qualify a police officer prosecuting criminal cases in magistrate courts. It should be recalled that most crimes that are taken to these courts are minor offences which do not attract more than 7 years jail term. Again, these police officers are usually not lawyers.

POLICE REPORT – It is a document issued by the police authority to show that the holder has made a report of a crime incident or loss of important documents or items, e.g. ATM cards, at a police station. The report usually contains the name of a complainant, the nature of crime committed or item lost and such other details. It may be a one-page document or more. It is often issued at a cost to be borne by the complainant. It should be noted that most hospitals do not treat accident victims or gunshot wounds unless this document is produced.

POWER OF ATTORNEY – It is a written authority given by one person (usually called principal) to another (otherwise known as agent) in order to empower the latter to act on behalf of the former. The agent, through *power of attorney*, may do a lot of things on behalf of the principal e.g. operating a bank account, running a business, holding title documents and initiating legal actions and so on. A *power of attorney* is automatically terminated upon the death of the giver.

PRAYER - This simply means the main purpose why a plaintiff is in court. In other words, it means what the plaintiff wants the court to do for him in terms of granting his request. For example, the *prayer* of a spouse who has filed an action for divorce is usually to get an order of court dissolving their marriage. The word *"prayer"* may be used interchangeably with relief or claim. It should be noted that whatever a party does not ask from court, he will not be given and whatever he asks, he must prove in order to get it.

PRECEDENT – This word may be used in two different ways. One, it may mean **JUDICIAL PRECEDENT** which has been previously explained. Two, it may mean a sample which could be a document being used as a guide to prepare another one of its kind. All the court papers which form part of this book towards the end are meant to serve as *precedents*.

PRE-ACTION NOTICE – It refers to a notice that is required by law in relation to some matters involving public bodies such as local governments and universities in which a claimant has to give to the other party concerned before initiating a court action. Where the claimant fails to give such notice, his action may be struck out for failing to comply with a condition precedent, provided that the other party raises an objection on the basis of the claimant's failure timely.

PRE-INCORPORATION CONTRACTS – These encompass contracts entered into by a company's promoter before the company is legally formed. Such contracts are usually not binding on the company once it comes into existence, except the company decides to ratify the contracts.

PRELIMINARY OBJECTION – It is a point of challenge raised against a case which rests mainly on non-compliance with a provision of law before the case is instituted in order to truncate such case at the early stage.

PREPONDERANCE OF EVIDENCE (BALANCE OF PROBABILITY) - This is the measure of evidence that a plaintiff in a civil case needs to produce in support of his case in order to have the court's judgement in his favour. It basically means a more credible and believable evidence in any case and any side that produces such evidence gets the judgement of the court. (Contrast: **PROOF BEYOND REASONABLE DOUBT**).

PREROGATIVE OF MERCY (also known as **PARDON**) – It is the power of a governor or the president to grant either conditional or total pardon to those who have been convicted of crimes whether they are still serving their punishments or they are ex-convicts. Once a person is granted pardon, especially if total, such person's criminal record is totally erased and the previous conviction cannot count against him anymore.

PRESUMPTION OF INNOCENCE – It simply means the right of a suspect to be seen as innocent until he is tried in a law court and found guilty in respect of a criminal allegation.

PRE-TRIAL CONFERENCE – It is a meeting before the commencement of trial between the judge, the lawyers and the parties involved in a case in order to narrow down the issues in dispute between the parties and explore possibility of settlement without proceeding to trial. The ultimate aim of this system is to hasten the process of determining cases in courts.

PRIMA FACIE – It means "on the surface." Usage – *"Reading through all the statements of witnesses to be called by the prosecution, I do not think a **prime facie** case of armed robbery is disclosed."*

PRINCIPAL – This is a person who appoints another person (otherwise known as agent) to act on his behalf. *Principal* and agent relationship is contractual and so each has rights and obligations to the other.

PRIVATE COMPANY – It is a company formed by a minimum of two persons but cannot, by law, have more than 50 members. It cannot raise capital from members of the public. Its name must end with "LTD" which means "Limited".

PRIVATE DOCUMENTS – These are documents issued by private individuals or companies including public companies. For the purpose of being used in courts, original copies of these documents are the only kind that is acceptable. However, on some occasions, their photocopies may be admitted if certain conditions are met.

PRIVITY OF CONTRACT – This is a principle which states that it is only a party to a contract that can enforce it. For example, **A** owes **B** some amount of money. Later **B** needs to travel outside the country but before he leaves, he instructs his wife, **C**, to collect the money owed him by **A** on his behalf and this arrangement is to the knowledge of **A**. If **A** pays the money as promised, very good, but if he does not, there is nothing which **C** on her own can do because the contract is between **A** and **B** not **B** and **C**. This is the essence of the principle of *privity of contract*.

PROBATION – This is a form of punishment imposed on persons who have been found guilty of a crime whereby they are allowed to stay in their community and are placed under the supervision of a probation officer for the purpose of monitoring their behaviour. They usually render certain services in the community where they stay. Apart from Lagos State[15], this form of punishment does not exist anywhere else in Nigeria.

PRO BONO – It means the performance of legal services by a lawyer to a person free of charge.

PROMOTERS – These are persons who set out and take steps to ensure that a company is formed. In some cases, *promoters* fade out once the company comes into being while on some other occasions, they may take up shares and become part of the owners of such company.

---

[15]. See, section 341 of the Administration of Criminal Justice Law of Lagos State, 2011.

PROMULGATION – It is a process by which a law is passed.

PROOF BEYOND REASONABLE DOUBT[16] – It is a standard of proof in a criminal case which is attained by the prosecution where the ingredients of a crime are proved to the satisfaction of court.

PROOF OF EVIDENCE – This is a compilation of documents which the prosecution has prepared in respect of a criminal case against a particular suspect. The *proof of evidence* usually contains a charge sheet, statements of witnesses as well as that of the suspect and a list of exhibits, if any.

PROOF OF SERVICE – It is a piece of evidence, usually documentary, to show that a party has been served with certain court papers or that a party is aware of the case before the court.

PROSECUTOR – This is a person, usually a state counsel, who brings a criminal charge against accused persons in courts and calls witnesses to prove the charge in order to get the accused persons punished for their crimes. *Prosecutor* may be used interchangeably with "prosecution".

PROXY – This is a practice where a member or non-member of a company is attending a meeting on behalf of a member who is unable to be present. A *proxy* can do whatever the absentee member has right to do, if he is around.

PUBLIC COMPANY – This is a company founded by a minimum of two persons and without any limit to the numerical strength of its membership. It may raise its capital through general members of the public and its name must end with "PLC" which stands for "Public Liability Company".

---

[16]. The principle of proof beyond reasonable doubt is premised on the basis that it is better to let ten accused persons go scot-free rather than punishing one innocent soul unjustifiably.

PUBLIC DOCUMENTS – These are documents issued by public bodies or documents kept in public places. It is an established principle that for the purpose of using such documents in courts it is their certified true copies that must be produced for court use. (See, **CERTIFIED TRUE COPY**). Examples of *public documents* are newspapers, records of public institutions e.g. Central Bank and so on.

PUBLIC INTEREST LITIGATION – This is a court action initiated by a person or a group of persons for the sake of protecting the interest of a particular individual or individuals who have suffered condemnable act of human rights abuse or to safeguard public interest in general. It is basically an action taken in the interest of others e.g. a recent action filed by a civil society organization asking the court to compel the law-makers (the National Assembly members) to disclose their salaries to Nigerians in view of the passage of the Freedom of Information Act.

PURCHASER – This word is normally used to qualify a buyer of any goods including landed property e.g. land.

Q

QUANTUM MERIUT – It is a remedy given in a case of breach of contract where an aggrieved party is awarded some compensation which equates with the degree of work or services that such party has performed in relation to the breached contract. This relief is usually granted where no specific amount is indicated to be paid to a party who has performed his obligations in respect of the contract to some extent.

QUASHING OF CHARGE – It is an application initiated by a suspect asking the court to strike out a criminal case against him on the basis that all the statements made by the prosecution's potential witnesses do not establish a tangible case against him. The aim of such application is to truncate the trial even before the suspect's plea is taken on the charge.

QUIC QUID PLANTATUR SOLO SOLO CEDIT – This is a principle of law which states that an owner of land owns everything beneath and above such land. However, in Nigeria, the law does not give ownership of mineral deposits found in a private individual land to the owner of such land. The ownership of mineral deposits resides with the federal government.

QUID PRO QUO – It means something for something. It is normally used to express the exchange of consideration (i.e. one of the valid elements of a contract) between parties to a contract. Usage – *"What is the **quid pro quo** for my supplying of this valuable information to your organization?"* (For more on this, see **CONSIDERATION** above).

QUORUM – It is the minimum number of members required to hold a meeting whether in a company, parliament or society. This means that if the required number is not met, a meeting cannot hold and if held, any decision made is invalid.

R

RAPE – It is a crime which is committed when a man has unlawful sexual intercourse with a woman or girl without her consent or with her consent obtained through inducement, threat of harm or impersonating her husband. When an underage girl (e.g. a girl below 11 years of age) is sexually assaulted, it is not *rape* but defilement which attracts, like rape, life imprisonment. The offence of rape is committed once a male organ penetrates a woman's vagina, irrespective of whether there is ejaculation or not. In Nigeria, rape can only be committed by a man and only a woman can be a victim.

However, a woman may be charged with rape if she aids a man to commit the offence. In some U.S states, rape can be committed by either a woman or a man[17].

RATIO DECIDENDI – This is the portion of a court judgement which deals with the main issue in contention between parties to a suit. It must be followed by lower courts whenever they are faced with similar situations in future cases. (Contrast: **OBITER DICTUM**).

REAL ESTATE/PROPERTY - It refers to immovable property such as land and houses.

REASONABLE WEAR AND TEAR – It is a kind of damage that may occur as a result of the use of property over a period of time. For instance, a tenant may not be held liable for damage that occurs in the apartment occupied by him as a consequence of the normal use of the property.

RECALL – It is a method of removing a law-maker from office before the expiration of his tenure. The right to remove a law-maker resides with the electorate.

RECALLING A WITNESS – This arises where a witness who has previously given evidence in respect of a matter in court needs to be

---

[17]. Rape in some states in the U.S is defined as *"A physical invasion of a sexual nature committed on a person under circumstances which are coercive. Whoever... knowingly causes another person to engage in a sexual act by threatening or placing that other person in fear (other than by threatening or placing that other person in fear that any person will be subjected to death, serious bodily injury, or kidnapping); or engages in a sexual act with another person if that other person is incapable of appraising the nature of the conduct; or physically incapable of declining participation in, or communicating willingness to engage in, that sexual act."* See, The US Code at Title 18, Part 1, Chapter 109A (2007), 2242 cited in Y.H. RAO and Y. R. RAO, "Criminal Trial" Fundamentals and Evidentiary Aspects 4th Edition Published by Wadhwa and Company Law Publishers, New Delhi, India, 2008.

called back for the purpose of giving additional evidence due to a new development in the same case.

RECESS – It is a yearly period when courts, especially superior courts, go on vacation. It usually commences in July and ends in September or early October.

RECEIVERSHIP – It is an order of court placing all property which is a subject of legal action under the control of an independent person known as a receiver in order to prevent the property from being dissipated or moved outside the jurisdiction of court. This order is usually made to protect the property of a company or business in respect of which there is a dispute.

RECITALS – These are statements in preliminary parts of legal documents that attempt to set out some important details or background information about a transaction which such documents cover. *Recitals* are commonly found in documents such as land sales agreement, deed, lease agreement, tenancy agreement and so on. For example, in a land sale agreement, *recitals* are used to briefly narrate how a vendor derives his title to the land being sold. Wordings in *recitals* may appear in this manner: *"WHEREAS the vendor became seized of the parcel of the land through inheritance from his late father, Chief Adagbamaku, under the Yoruba native law and customs"*.

RECOGNIZANCE – This constitutes a monetary assurance given by a person (technically known as surety) in exchange for the grant of bail to a suspect. The implication of entering into recognizance for a suspect on bail is that the surety is likely to pay a specified amount of money regarded as *recognizance* to the coffers of government, if the suspect runs away (i.e. to jump bail).

RECORD OF PROCEEDINGS – This represents a compilation of everything that takes place in respect of a case before a lower court which is now being sent to a higher court for the purpose of enabling the higher court to deal with an appeal that has been filed against the lower court's judgement. Record of proceedings usually contains all the court papers filed at the lower court, verbatim report of evidence given, arguments of lawyers and judgement of the lower court.

REDEMPTION – This represents the rights of a mortgagor to reclaim the mortgaged property. It is for this reason that it is commonly said that "once a mortgage, always a mortgage". It is rare for a mortgagor to lose this right to redeem the mortgaged property and if he has to lose it, then it must be through a court order.

REDUNDANCY - It is a situation where the available workforce outweighs the volume of work that is to be done in which case an employer may have to reduce the number of employees by terminating the appointment of some of them.

RE-EXAMINATION – In giving evidence in courts, witnesses do so through three different ways and they are examination-in-chief, cross examination and re-examination. The first two have been explained above. *Re-examination* comes last and it means a process of questions and answers which takes place between a lawyer and a witness who must have previously given evidence under cross-examination and is now being questioned in order to clear the air on one or few things which he said while being cross-examined that are not clear enough. Unless there is an issue which arises under cross-examination that needs to be clarified, there may not be need for *re-examination*.

REGISTRAR – This is a court official who assists a magistrate or judge in the performance of his duties. A *registrar* reads out cases before the court, maintains the diary of the court and adjourns cases when the court is not sitting.

REINSTATEMENT - It is an act or a court order returning a dismissed employee to his job after the court has found that his dismissal is unlawful. This kind of order is commonly granted in respect of employments in public sector and not where an employee works in a private sector. Even if an employee working for a private employer is unlawfully dismissed, all the court would do is to award damages in favour of such employee rather than ordering a reinstatement as it is often said that "a willing employee cannot be forced on an unwilling employer."

RELEVANCY – It is a principle of law which regulates the nature of evidence to be given in a case in court. It requires parties or witnesses to give evidence of only facts or state of things that are connected to the case on trial. Evidence on facts not connected to the issue before the court will be rejected.

RE-LISTING – There are occasions that a plaintiff's suit may be struck out by a court especially if it appears that the plaintiff is no longer interested in following up his case. If a plaintiff's case is struck out this way, one of the options open to such party is to either forget about his case or to take steps in order to bring it back before the court. Where he opts to bring it back, the application which he needs to get this done is known as *re-listing*.

REMAND HOME[18] – It is an institution where juvenile offenders between 8 and 16 years, who are too young to go to regular prisons, may be detained.

REPEAL – It is a legislative act of cancelling a law which means that such law can no longer be binding on the people.

REPRESENTATIVE ACTION - It is a case filed by a group of people who have a common cause. For example, a case filed by a number of former staff of PHCN challenging the wrongful manner in which their employment was terminated is a good specimen of a *representative action*. (Compare: **CLASS ACTION**).

REPRODUCTION WARRANT – It is an order of court directed at the prisons authority commanding the production of a specified

---

[18]. For more details, read this – "Bankole weeps at remand home" – http://news2.onlinenigeria.com/latest-addition/87437-bankole-weeps-at-remand-home.html (visited on 28th December, 2013).

prison inmate in court on a particular date so that he may be present in court to undergo his trial.

REPUDIATION OF CONTRACT - It means a rejection of a contract as a result of a breach committed by the other party.

RESERVED JUDGEMENT – This arises where a judgement in a case which has been concluded is postponed to another date instead of being given at the moment.

RESIDENCE PERMIT – It is an official document giving permission to a foreigner who intends to stay in Nigeria for more than three months.

RES IPSA LOQUITOR – It means "the fact or thing speaks for itself." Usage - *"The fact that you are a lawyer is **res ipsa loquitor** because you actually speak like one."*

RES JUDICATA – This is a principle which states that once a civil matter has been decided by a court, people affected by such case cannot start the same case all over again before the same court or another court which is of equal status as the former one, unless the matter goes on appeal. This is designed to prevent a situation where a case which has been decided would be commenced afresh.

RESOLUTIONS – These are decisions taken by companies in respect of different subject-matters at their general meetings. *Resolutions* may be written, special or ordinary.

RESPONDENT – This is a party who has a favourable judgement on his side from a lower court but which is now being challenged on appeal before a higher court. It may also be used to refer to a person responding to an application before any court.

RESTITUTIO IN INTEGRUM – It means to restore a person to his former position. It is a relief usually granted in a case of breach of contract. It is an order of court restoring a victorious party in respect of a contract to the position he would have been if the breach had not occurred.

RETAINER (also known as **RETAINER** or **RETAINERSHIP AGREEMENT**) - It is a kind of agreement that exists between a lawyer and a client whereby the latter hires the former to provide him legal services from time to time. The agreement drawn up in this kind of relationship would spell out the nature of services to be provided, the duration of the relationship, the expenses and other relevant matters. A lawyer retained in this manner may loosely be referred to as a family lawyer, club lawyer, personal lawyer and so on. However, this agreement does not create employer and employee relationship.

RETRACTION – It is a denial of a confessional statement made prior to court proceedings by a suspect in the course of his trial. By *retraction,* a suspect is saying he did not make a confessional statement which the prosecution claims to have been made by him at the police station.

RETRENCHMENT- It means the termination of an employee due to economic downturn.

RETRIAL – This is an order of a higher court returning a case which has been previously concluded by a lower court to the same former court in order to re-open it and commence it all over again.

RETROACTIVE LAW (also known as **RETROSPECTIVE LAW**) – This is a law made to have effect from the past. This form of legislation may be made in civil matters but in relation to criminal law, it is totally prohibited which means no person can be charged for a crime created under a new law when an act constituting the crime under the new law has been done in the past at a time that such act is not a crime at all. For example, **A** and **B** got married two years ago as gay couple in Nigeria when there was no law criminalising such union. Unless their marriage continues to this moment, they cannot be held liable for the marriage they had contracted then under the new law on gay marriage.

RETURN DAY (DATE): This refers to another day in which a matter is coming up before a court and by which the other party is expected to appear in court. This is usually the case where an order for ex parte application has been granted.

RIGHT OF ACTION – This is the legal basis to bring and maintain an action in court. A factual basis (otherwise known as **CAUSE OF ACTION**) must have first arisen before a party can approach a court in order to exercise his *right of action*.

ROOT OF TITLE – This refers to the origin of one's ownership of a particular property. One may have to trace his origin of ownership of a plot of land to the person who sells the land to him.

RULES OF COURT – Every court especially from the High Court to the Supreme Court has its rules which regulate the conduct of cases before it. These rules must be adhered to in filing cases up to the point of hearing witnesses until judgement is given. Any person having a case in court ought to be familiar with the rules of the affected court. An example of *rules of court* is the Oyo State High Court (Civil Procedure) Rules, 2010.

S

SEARCH WARRANT – It is an official document which permits a police officer to search the premises of a person who has been suspected to have committed a crime so as to retrieve pieces of evidence for the purpose of prosecuting him.

SECONDMENT - This is a situation where an employee is posted outside his regular place of work by his employer usually on a temporary arrangement.

SELF-RECOGNIZANCE – In granting bails by courts to suspects, certain conditions are usually imposed in order to ensure that suspects return to court for their trials. However, there are occasions where such conditions may not be imposed if a suspect is a well-known individual in the society who is not likely to run away, especially if a minor offence is being alleged.

SENIOR ADVOCATES OF NIGERIA[19]- It is the highest rank and honour that can be conferred on a practising lawyer in Nigeria. It is meant to honour lawyers who have performed excellently well in courtroom advocacy and law teachers who have made outstanding contributions to the advancement of legal knowledge. Senior Advocates do not appear in lower courts such as magistrate and customary courts. However, some people have called for the abolition of the rank in Nigeria because, as they argue, it promotes division among lawyers and its award is[20] not based on merits. They argue that it has been abolished in Ghana and South-Africa, while nothing of such exists in America at all.

SENTENCING – It is the point at which a court imposes a definite punishment on an accused person who must have first been found guilty of an offence in the same judgment. (See, **CONVICTION**).

SERVICE CONTRACT – This term may be used in two slightly different ways. One, it may refer to a relationship between two parties where one repairs some appliances or products e.g. car, factory machines and so on over a period of time and for a specific

---

[19]. For more details, see the article "HOW TO BECOME SAN" attached as an addendum to this book in Section D below. In England, from where the institution of SAN came, its equivalent is called Queen's Counsel (QC).

[20]. See, "Creating a class distinction in the temple of justice is injustice- Pa Gomez", http://dailyindependentnig.com/2014/03/creating-a-class-distinction-in-the-temple-of-justice-is-injustice-pa-gomez/ (accessed on 21st March, 2014).

amount of fees which may be in form of salary to be paid by the other party who is the beneficiary of the service rendered. Secondly, it may refer to a relationship between directors and a company where the former work as employees of the latter by making their expertise available to the company in exchange for an agreed remuneration. The contract is usually protected by the company's articles of association and the law.

SERVICE OCCUPANCY/TENANCY - This is a situation where an employee is given accommodation by his employer in which the tenancy of the employee terminates simultaneously with the termination of his employment. This type of tenant or occupier is not entitled to normal quit notice that regular tenants must be given in order to eject them. This tenancy is common with company and tertiary institution employments where employees live in their employers' quarters.

SERVICE OUTSIDE JURISDICTION – This is a situation where a court paper issued by a court sitting in one state has to be served on persons residing in another state. In order to effect service of a court paper in another state, special procedure is usually adopted for doing so. This applies to papers issued by state courts and not federal courts such as the Federal High **Court.**

SET OFF – This is a form of monetary claim filed by a defendant in the same suit where he is sued by a plaintiff for recovery of debt or damages and in response to the plaintiff's case, the defendant is asking the court to give an order deducting what he owes the plaintiff from what the latter is also owing him. For example, **A** files an action to claim for the payment of money due to him from **B**. **B** in responding to **A**'s suit, on the other hand, is asking the court to deduct what he owes **A** from what **A** is owing him which may be from another transaction. The claim that **B** is making in this regard qualifies as *set-off*.

SETTING DOWN – It is an application requesting a court to fix a matter for the purpose of taking arguments or testimony of witnesses.

SETTLEMENT OUT OF COURT – It is a situation where a dispute is resolved not through a court judgement but rather through a process of negotiation and compromise between parties. Courts also encourage this kind of conflict resolution methods and a case before a court may still be resolved amicably even without withdrawing it from the court. (See, CONSENT JUDGEMENT).

SEVERALLY LIABLE - If two or more persons are *severally liable*, it means each person has a share of liability which is individually borne and not collectively. For example, if a group of persons, on one hand, enters into a contract with another person, on the other hand, in which there is several liability clause and a member of the group fails to perform his portion of the contract, it is only the person who fails to perform that is liable to the other party and not all the members of the group. For a plaintiff, a claim for damages in which defendants are made jointly and *severally liable* is better than either being made jointly or *severally liable*. (Contrast: **JOINT LIABILITY**).

SHARE CAPITAL – It means the portion of a company's financial assets contributed by members of the company with which the company does its business and pays the members some returns.

SHAREHOLDER – This is a person who has contributed money to the share capital of a company and whose name appears on the company's register of members. He also has right to attend the company's meeting. He is basically a co-owner of a company.

SHERIFF - This is a court official who is usually deployed to enforce a court judgement.

SINE DIE – It means indefinitely. A case may have to be adjourned without giving it a specific date in which case it will be said that it is adjourned *sine die*.

SMALL CLAIMS – This describes civil cases which may be commenced in a magistrate court in view of small amount of damages or money that is involved. Any civil suit in which a party is claiming for the recovery of less than a million naira debts or damages is regarded as *small **claims.***

SOLICITOR - In England, *solicitors* are lawyers who do pre-court preparations and render other legal services such as drafting of court processes, contractual documents and other corporate transactions. A *solicitor* does not represent clients in courts. So in England, there is a distinction between a solicitor and a barrister but in Nigeria, it is not so. Here, a lawyer is both a solicitor and a barrister.

SOLICITOR-GENERAL – This is the most senior career officer in the Ministry of Justice who must also be a lawyer. He serves as the administrative head of the Ministry; hence, he is usually both the *Solicitor-General* and Permanent-Secretary.

SPECIFIC PERFORMANCE – It is an order of court given in a case bordering on contract where an award of damages will not be just in the circumstance but rather a command asking a party to carry out his obligation in respect of the contract.

STANDARD OF PROOF - It is the measure of evidence as fixed by law which a party has to produce in his case in order to obtain a favourable judgement. For instance, in a criminal case, the prosecution must prove its case against an accused person beyond reasonable doubt so as to find him guilty of the alleged offence, while in a civil case, a party's evidence must be more credible or believable than that of his opponent in order to have the court's judgement in his favour.

STAND-DOWN – A case, having been first called in court, may be put on hold while other cases are attended to in order to return to the first case later. To stand a case down is not the same as adjourning the matter because a case stood down will still come up before the court on the same day.

STARE DECISIS - It means "standing by former decisions". This principle is closely connected to judicial precedent. While judicial precedent enjoins lower courts to follow previous decisions of higher courts in deciding similar cases before them (i.e. by ensuring that like cases are treated alike), *stare decisis* states that once a previous judgement of a higher court is similar to a case before a lower court, the latter is authoritatively bound to follow such previous decision of the former.

STALE CHEQUE – This is a cheque that has become expired, having been issued for more than six months without the money on it being paid.

STATE COUNSEL – Lawyers who serve in the Ministry of Justice, whether at the state or federal level are usually called *State Counsel*. In some states, they are also addressed as Legal or Law Officers.

STATEMENT OF CLAIM – It is a document (court paper) which contains facts (story) concerning a plaintiff's case in court. (For more details, see FACTS above).

STATEMENT OF DEFENCE – It is the response of a defendant to the plaintiff's case in which the defendant denies either in part or in full the facts in the plaintiff's statement of claims.

STATUS QUO – It means to keep a state of things as it is. Once a case is filed in respect of a dispute, it is usually expected of parties to stop further action on anything having to do with the subject-matter in court until the court decides.

STATUS QUO ANTE – This refers to a state of things as at the time an action is filed in court. This can be illustrated this way – **A** is an employee of **E**. When **A** realizes that certain steps being taken by **E** are aimed at easing him out of his employment, he immediately rushes to court to seek for an order to prevent **E** from completing what he is already doing. As at the time **E** is served with the court papers filed by **A**, the latter has not been disengaged. If **E** goes ahead to disengage **A** in spite of his knowledge of the case in court, the court may order **E** to revert to the position which **A** was prior to the court action. This is *status quo ante*.

STATUTE-BARRED ACTION – This is an action being filed in court outside the time limit allowed for it by law. For example, the law requires a suit seeking to challenge an act of a public servant to be brought within 3 months of the performance of such official act. If an action is now commenced after the expiration of this time limit, such action will be struck out for being *statute-barred*.

STATUTE LAW/STATUTORY AUTHORITY – When a lawyer refers a court of law to, for example, section 6 (b) of the Armed Robbery and Firearms (Special Provisions) Act, Cap. R. 11 Vol. 14, Laws of the Federation of Nigeria, 2004, a *statutory authority* is said to have been cited because this law is not a court decision but a law made by the law-makers. Laws made by legislators at any level of governments are regarded as statute law or *statutory authority*, especially when they are being used in courts.

STATUTE OF LIMITATION – This is a law which provides for the time limit within which a case may be filed in court. If the case is brought to court outside the time set, then a court will lack jurisdiction to preside over it because the case would have been statute-barred. For example, a case which borders on the enforcement of a formal contract should be filed within twelve years when a breach of contract occurs or within six years in respect of an informal contract. (Compare: **STATUTE-BARRED ACTION**).

STATUTORY EMPLOYMENT – This is a form of employment contract at any level of governments in which the relationship between the employees and the employers is governed by law. The law sets out the rights and duties of each party to the relationship. This is the case of civil service employment. In this kind of relationship, the employer, in particular, cannot terminate an employee's contract without following the laid down procedure and if it fails to do so, then an order of court reinstating such employee may be granted. Courts however rarely reinstate wrongfully dismissed employees in private employment.

STAY OF EXECUTION - It is an application seeking to stop a judgement from being carried out because of an appeal that is filed before a higher court.

STRICTO SENSO – It means that something e.g. a law or procedure must be followed strictly. In other words, a law may have to be followed to the letters.

STRICT LIABILITY (known as **STRICT LIABILITY OFFENCES** in criminal law)- It is a liability which may arise either in a criminal or civil case. It means that a person is strictly liable for a criminal act, for instance, even if he does not have intention to commit a particular crime e.g. in a case of manslaughter. All that is required to be proved here is that an accused person is the one that kills the deceased, though without intention to kill. Other examples of strict liability offences include smoking of Indian hemp, unlawful possession of arms, over-speeding and sales of counterfeit drugs. However, strict liability crimes are not as many as those other offences that require the proof of intention (i.e. *mens rea*) in the Nigerian criminal law and even when created, they are mostly minor offences that carry light punishments. In a civil case, on the other hand, a defendant may be held liable for a legal wrong, even though the wrong occurred not due to his fault. If, for instance, a person keeps a dangerous animal e.g. lion in his premises and the animal escapes and injures another person, the keeper is strictly liable even if he does everything necessary to prevent the animal from escaping.

STRIKING OUT A CASE – A case is said to be struck out when it is removed from the list of cases before a court. A case that is struck out has not been determined on its merits and may be brought back before the same court through relisting[21]. (Contrast: **DISMISSING A CASE**).

SUBJECT TO CONTRACT – This phrase is commonly used to show that a contract is still under negotiation. When it is found on a document, it means such contract has not been finalized and is not binding on the parties yet.

SUB JUDICE – This means a matter that is already before a court. Once a matter is in court, it constitutes a violation of this principle to subject the same matter to indiscriminate media or public discussion. Further discussions on the subject are supposed to be minimal, if not totally suspended, until the case is finally decided by the court.

SUBPOENA – It is a court order requesting especially a witness to appear before a court for the purpose of giving evidence. Subpoena is of two types. The two are *subpoena ad testificandum* and *subpoena duces tecum*. Subpoena ad testificandum requires a witness to give oral evidence in court which may include tendering of documents and it may not. Subpoena duces tecum, on the other hand, only requires a witness to tender a document(s) without giving oral evidence at all.

SUBSTANTIAL JUSTICE – This is a concept which enjoins courts to look at the merit of litigants' cases instead of truncating their cases because of technical defects in the manner they have presented them. When a court looks at the heart of a party's case and refuses to be distracted by a defect in format, it will be said that the court is doing *substantial justice*.

SUBSTANTIVE CASE – This refers to a main case and not some off-shoots of such case. For example, if **A** is being tried for the murder of **B** and **A** in the course of his trial decides to bring an application for his bail, his trial itself is the substantive case while the application for bail is regarded as interlocutory case. So also an

---

[21]. See, RELISTING above.

application brought in a civil case which is meant to restrain a party from continuing to develop a plot of land until the court decides who owns the land between the two parties in court in its final judgement can be described as an interlocutory application (or interlocutory order or injunction), while the issue of ownership of land is the substantive case. (See, **INTERLOCUTORY APPLICATION**).

SUBSTITUTED SERVICE - This is a situation which arises where a party to a suit cannot be served with court papers in person. As a result, an order of court must be obtained in order to serve him through some other possible means e.g. by posting the papers to him (especially where a defendant resides outside Nigeria), by pasting the papers on the wall of his last known address or by advertising the papers in the national dailies.

SUMMARY JUDGEMENT – It refers to a judgment given in a court proceeding without going through full-fledged trial.

SUMMARY OFFENCE – This comprises minor offences for which punishments are usually below one year jail term or a small amount of money as fine and in which case, if a suspect admits his guilt in the open court, a magistrate court may forthwith convict and sentence him. Examples of offences in this category are breach of the peace, driving against traffic light, violations of environmental sanitation regulations and so on.

SUI GENERIS – It means something which is unique and of its own kind.

SUI JURIS – It means one who has legal capacity i.e. not suffering from any legal disability whether on account of age or mind.

SUO MOTU – It means an issue raised by a court on its own. Whenever a court raises an issue *suo motu*, it must give parties opportunity to express their views on such issue.

SUPERIOR COURTS OF RECORD - This refers to those courts from the level of a state high court to the Supreme Court level. In all these courts, the principle of judicial precedent operates.

SUPRA – It means "above." It is normally used in legal writing to refer to a case or statutory authority that has earlier been mentioned in a text, so as to avoid full repetition of details in subsequent reference.

SURETY – It means a person who gives assurance of another person's good behaviour and where the other person fails to behave as assured then the person giving assurance will be held liable. A *surety* is normally required in relation to a suspect who is to be released on bail.

SUSPECT – This is a person who is alleged to have committed a crime or crimes. A person ceases to be called a suspect the moment he is charged to court for his trial and at that point, he becomes an accused person or defendant.

T

TAINTED WITNESS – This is a witness in a case who appears to have a personal interest to serve through the manner in which he testifies. This situation often arises where, in a criminal case, a person, who ought to have been charged in the same case in which he gives evidence but is not charged by the prosecution in order to elicit vital evidence from him necessary to convict a suspect or suspects, gives evidence in court. He may be classified as *tainted witness* if he appears desperate to implicate the suspect by all means.

TECHNICAL JUSTICE – This phrase is often used to describe a kind of judgement which is given, not based on the merits of a party's case but on mere failure to comply with some rules. For example, **A** is a tenant who pays his rents yearly while **B** is the landlord. As at March, 2013, **A** has not paid his rents for the year 2013 which he ought to have paid since January 1st 2013. **B**, being fed up of demanding for the rents without positive response from **A**, decided to eject **A** from his premises by serving him a quit notice of 5 days instead of the clear 7 days before he would have to go to court. So at the expiration of 5 days, **B** filed an action against **A** in court. It took the court four months to conduct the case and give judgement. The court decided that the quit notice served on **A** was not proper and therefore **B**'s case failed. This kind of decision is an example of technical justice because the judgement did not decide whether **A** ought to pack out or not but that **B** did not take the right steps before coming to the court. The judgement did not also take into consideration the fact that **A** is in arrears of rents while **B** is being deprived of legitimate earnings.

TENANCY - This is an agreement which involves the letting of an apartment, whether for residential or commercial purpose, by a person called tenant from another person called landlord who is usually the owner of the apartment or another person who acts as his agent. To create a valid tenancy agreement (or popularly referred to as landlord and tenant relationship), there must be a specified amount of money to be paid by the tenant as rents and the duration of tenancy must be specific which must be under a period of 3 years because once a tenancy is up to 3 years, it is no longer a tenancy relationship but a lease. (See, **LEASE** above).

TENANCY IN COMMON - This refers to property owned by more than one person but with a distinct portion of the property allotted to each owner. For instance, if **A** and **B** own a storey building in common, it means one of them i.e. either **A** or **B** will own the ground floor while the other person will have the first floor. Each owner can do whatever he likes with his own share but not anything that will negatively affect the interest of the other owner. (Compare: **JOINT TENANCY**).

TENANCY AT SUFFRANCE- This is a tenant who is occupying an apartment even when his tenancy has expired and who, by law, is only entitled to 7 days' "owner's intention to recover premises" in order to recover the premises from him. It should be pointed out that the tenant holds the premises over, though without the consent of the landlord.

TENANT AT WILL- This refers to a tenant who is occupying an apartment even when his tenancy has expired and who, by law, is only entitled to 7 days' quit notice in order to eject him from premises occupied by him. It should be pointed out that the tenant holds the premises over with the understanding of the landlord.

TERMINATION - This implies an act of bringing a contract to an end. For instance, in a contract of employment, letters of appointment usually indicate how either the employer or the employee may terminate the contract. An employee may terminate his working relationship with an employer by simply giving the employer a month's notice or any length of notice depending on the agreement between them and likewise the employer may terminate it by giving the required notice. An employee whose employment is terminated is, unlike a dismissed staff, entitled to his terminal benefits.

TERMS OF SETTLEMENT - These are issues on which agreement has been reached by certain persons and in which a document has been prepared to express such areas of agreement. An agreement made this way is usually binding on persons affected by the document. This kind of document containing areas of agreement is commonly prepared where parties to a dispute are settling their differences through amicable means. Compare: **CONSENT JUDGMENT** and **SETTLEMENT OUT OF COURT**.

TESTIMONY – It refers to statements made by a witness in a case under oath in which he may be punished if it turns out that some statements are deliberately made to mislead a court. The word *"testimony"* may be used interchangeably with "evidence".

THE SILK - It is used to refer to Senior Advocates of Nigeria collectively or an individual Senior Advocate of Nigeria. (See, **INNER BAR**).

TITLE DOCUMENTS – These are documents which prove one's ownership over certain property e.g. Certificate of Occupancy (C of O).

TORTFEASOR – This refers to a person who commits a civil wrong such as negligence, defamation and other forms of tort.

TRADE DISPUTES - These are conflicts which have to do with the relationship between employers and employees or among employees or employers. The disputes may relate to the conditions of service, rights of employees to form unions, implementations of agreements between the two sides, wrongful terminations and so on.

TRADEMARK – It is a word, phrase, symbol, design or label which distinguishes goods or products of one party from those of others. A *trademark* which is registered enjoys legal protection to the extent that if violated, the owner of the *trademark* may sue to restrain the other person from continuous use of the *trademark* and also to claim damages. While *trademark* is protected by statutes, passing off is protected by case law. (See, **PASSING OFF**).

TRIAL COURT – It refers to a court handling a matter. It may be used interchangeably with trial judge in some cases. Usually, it refers to a court of first instance hearing a case as opposed to an appellate court e.g. the Court of Appeal. Examples of trial court or court of first instance, on the other hand, are Magistrate and High Courts.

TRIAL DATE - It is a day on which a case is slated for the hearing of witnesses' evidence to be commenced or arguments of lawyers to be taken.

TRIAL DE NOVO – It is a situation where a case that is almost completed has to be started afresh. *De Novo* itself means to start something afresh.

TRIAL WITHIN TRIAL – It is a mini-trial conducted in a criminal trial whenever a suspect is challenging the use of his confessional statement on the basis that he did not make it voluntarily. The court must hold this trial in order to determine whether the statement was obtained voluntarily or not before proceeding with the main trial.

TRIBUNAL- It is a body created by law to perform judicial-like function. A tribunal is not a court because it may be headed by a non-lawyer or have non-lawyers as members and it is commonly established to fast-track the course of justice. The Town Planners Disciplinary Tribunal, the Medical and Dental Practitioners Disciplinary Tribunal and many disciplinary committees are examples of tribunals[22].

TRITE – It means something that is certain or settled. This is commonly used by lawyers to express a point or an area of law that is clear and not contentious. Usage - *"It is **trite** that a criminal case must be proved beyond reasonable doubt."*

U

UBERIMAE FIDEI – It means utmost good faith. It is a principle which is usually followed in insurance contracts where a party taking up an insurance policy is required to make full and honest disclosure of information related to the transaction.

UBI JUS IBI REMEDIUM – It means "where there is injury, there is a remedy." What this implies is that whenever a person suffers a legal injury, there is always a relief at law.

---

[22]. For more on the meaning of a tribunal, see Chukkol K. S., "The Scope and Extent of Disciplinary Powers of Tertiary Institutions in Nigeria: Misconduct Vs Criminal Law" in Contemporary Issues in Nigerian Law: Legal Essays in Honour of Hon. Justice Umaru Faruk Abdullahi, CON. 2006. Kanam S. M. G. and Madaki A.M. (Eds.) Zaria: Ahmadu Bello University. Pages 447 to 448.

ULTRA VIRES – This refers to an act which is not within the scope of a person's authority. A company may be said to act *ultra vires* where it does things not covered by its memorandum of association or authorized by the general meeting.

UNDUE INFLUENCE – This constitutes a situation where a contract cannot be said to have been created through the freewill of the parties to the contract. This may occur when parties to a contract are not of equal bargaining power or social status to the extent that one exercises pressure on the other party in order to create the contract. Contract between a lawyer and his clients, guardians and their wards, spiritual leaders and their followers and so on may give cause for suspicion especially if the benefit of the contract tilts more to one side. *Undue influence*, if successfully proved, may nullify a contract because contracts are supposed to reflect voluntary wishes of the parties.

UNENFORCEABLE CONTRACT – It refers to a contract that, by law, must be in writing and if it is not, it cannot be enforced e.g. a contract of guarantee, hire purchase, a lease and so on.

UNILATERAL CONTRACT – It is an agreement made by a person with the whole world. It means the agreement or contract may be accepted by whoever is interested. This may be illustrated by a person who promises to give a specified sum of money to anybody that finds his lost Alsatian dog and returns it to his house. The implication of this kind of promise is that there is nobody to whom the offer is directed and nobody needs to signify his intention to accept before he performs it. The finding and returning of the dog in this regard constitute both acceptance and performance of the offer and whoever does that is entitled to the promised money.

UNLIQUIDATED DAMAGES – This is a kind of damages that is usually demanded in a civil case bordering on a tortious wrong e.g. defamation. An *unliquidated damages* lies within the discretion of a court to determine how much to grant to a party.

UPHELD - This refers to a situation where a higher court agrees with a judgement given by a lower court in respect of which the higher court has entertained an appeal and arrives at the same result like the lower court.

UPTURNING - This is a judgment of a higher court setting aside a lower court's judgment in respect of a matter. For instance, a party may lose a case before the Court of Appeal and therefore files an appeal against such judgment to the Supreme Court in which the latter court now gives a different judgment in favour of the party appealing.

V

VACATION JUDGE – This is a judge who is working while other judges have proceeded on annual recess. This judge is expected to attend to only emergency or urgent matters e.g. applications for bails. He works during the vacation period and proceeds on leave when others resume.

VENDOR – It is commonly used to qualify a seller of any good including landed property.

VETO – It refers to the powers of a governor or the president to prevent a bill that has been passed by the law-makers from becoming a law by refusing to give his assent. However, if a bill is not assented to within a prescribed length of time, the law makers may override the *veto* of the executive.

VICARIOUS LIABILITY – This arises where a person has to bear another person's liability because of the relationship that exists between them. For example, a principal is liable for the default of his agent while acting on his instructions.

VOID CONTRACT – It is a contract that cannot be enforced at all because it may either be lacking in vital elements that make a contract valid or a party does not have legal capacity to enter into it at all. For example, a contract of loan entered into by an underage person i.e. a person below 21 years is void.

VOIDABLE CONTRACT – It is a contract which, on the face of it, is valid until it is set aside at the instance of a party who has right to do so. For example, if a drunken person enters into a contract in his state of drunkenness, he may set it aside soon after he regains consciousness. Such contract is voidable but not void *ab initio*.

VOLENTI NON FIT INJURIA – It is a Latin phrase which means that a person who consents to a risk cannot complain. In other words, it means that where a person has fore-knowledge of likely risk which may follow his action, he may not be able to seek legal redress if the risk occurs.

W

WANT OF DILIGENT PROSECUTION - This means either that the prosecution is unable to produce its witnesses in court as a result of which a case cannot be heard or that the prosecution is not serious about calling its witnesses. Any of these possibilities may compel a court to strike out the prosecution's case. When a case is struck out this way, it means that a suspect would be discharged but not acquitted. If the prosecution later puts its house in order, the suspect may be re-arrested and tried. This may also apply to a civil case. If a plaintiff is unserious about his case, the case may be struck out for lack of diligent prosecution.

WARRANT OF ARREST - It is a paper issued by a court or a Justice of the Peace which commands the arrest of a specified person.

WARRANT OF COMMITTAL - It is an order of court by which a person accused of a crime is admitted into prison by prison administrators.

WARRANTY – These are terms usually inserted in a document to show that a party inserting those terms is bound to carry out his promises when occasions indicated arise. For example, it is common in sales of electrical appliances, vehicles and some other products that their manufacturers would give assurances to their customers to return products bought in case there is any damage within a specified period of time which usually ranges from six months to one year.

WATCHING BRIEF – In a criminal case, victims of crimes do not need to employ their own lawyers because the State would have stepped into their shoes to prosecute offenders on their behalf. However, a victim who wishes may still employ a lawyer who can only appear in court, possibly provide some assistance to the prosecuting police officer or government lawyer as the case may be, watch the trial and report back to the victim. But he cannot be heard by the court. So a lawyer employed by a victim in this way is said to hold a *watching brief*. He can only be seen by the court; he cannot be heard, though he may announce his appearance in the case. However, a lawyer holding a watching brief may also be heard with the permission of the court, especially if he has an observation or information which may assist the court.

WHITE PAPER - *(also known as **GOVERNMENT'S WHITE PAPER**)* It represents a decision taken by government on a report of a panel or commission of enquiry set up by the same government to look into a particular matter. In other words, it may be referred to as the official documentation made on a report submitted to government by a panel or commission e.g. the government's White Paper on Oputa Panel of 1999.

WILL – It is a legal document written by a person called testator in which he states how he wants his assets shared after his death among his chosen beneficiaries. For more details on the subject of wills, see my book, *How to Write Your Will with Ease*.

WINDING UP - It is a process by which the lifespan of a company is brought to an end. Once a company is wound up, it ceases to exist.

WITHOUT PREJUDICE - The phrase is usually inserted on letters to show that concessions, admissions and compromises made, while potential litigants are negotiating settlements, are not expected to bind them in case a court action is later instituted due to failure to settle a dispute amicably. Usually, letters marked "without prejudice" are not admissible in the course of litigation, unless it is shown that the phrase is not used in connection with genuine settlement process.

WITNESS BOX – It is a box, usually wooden, in which people giving evidence in any case stand in courts to testify. It is commonly located at the right hand side of a judge or magistrate.

WITNESS SUMMONS – It is an official document issued by a court directed to a specific person in which the person is commanded to appear in court at a specified date and venue for the purpose of giving evidence in a case. Disobeying a *witness summons* constitutes a contempt of court which may be punished by the court.

WORK-TO-RULE – It is a form of industrial action in which workers, though they are not on full-fledged strike, are working at a slow pace. In other words, workers are only performing skeletal operations.

WORK PERMIT – It is an official document which gives a non-Nigerian permission to take up a job in the country among the list of specified jobs for foreign workers.

WRIT OF POSSESSION - It is a court order which empowers a Sheriff to throw out a tenant's property in order to forcefully deliver a vacant apartment to a landlord after the latter must have earlier obtained a court order ejecting the tenant from the apartment. If a tenant voluntarily packs out of his rented apartment after an order ejecting him is served on him or he becomes aware of it, then the need for a writ of possession would not arise.

WRONGFUL DISMISSAL - This is a situation where an employee is dismissed without following the terms of his engagement which are binding on both the employee and the employer.

Y

YOUR LORDSHIP - This is used to address judges in Nigeria and many other countries formerly colonised by Britain, especially those judges from the high court level to the Supreme Court. They may also be addressed as "My Lord" or "His Lordship". In India, however, it is no longer mandatory to address judges from the high court upwards as "Your Lordship" or "My Lord" as the Supreme Court of the country has ruled that what is important is to address judges with respect and not necessarily by holding on to the traditional style of address. Therefore, it is not compulsory to call judges "Your Lordship" and the likes. There is nothing like "HER LORDSHIP" or "HER LADYSHIP" at this level because female judges are also treated as if they are males.

YOUR WORSHIP - Magistrates are addressed as "Your Worship" and they may also be addressed as "Your Honour" but it is not proper to address those among them who are women as "Your Lady" or "My Lady".

About the Book

This book explains legal terms in plain English, devoid of legal jargons for non-lawyers to read and understand.

About the Author

Kehinde Adegbite is a lawyer and a senior member of the Nigerian Bar. His experience cuts across both the private and official Bars. He is a renowned writer reputed for simplifying the knowledge of law for all to read and understand.

He is the author of *How to Write Your Will with Ease, Learning the Law in Nigeria, and What the Law Says about: Marriage and Divorce*. His books, though useful for lawyers, are written essentially for non-lawyers.

Visit the author's blog- www.kehindeadegbite.com.ng
Contact him - Email: barrykehinde@yahoo.co.uk
    Facebook: https://web.facebook.com/barrykehinde
    Twitter: https://twitter.com/barrykehinde

www.ingramcontent.com/pod-product-compliance
Lightning Source LLC
Chambersburg PA
CBHW072052230526
45479CB00010B/688